Killing It

Killing It

AN ENTREPRENEUR'S GUIDE TO KEEPING
YOUR HEAD WITHOUT LOSING YOUR HEART

SHERYL O'LOUGHLIN

HARPER
BUSINESS

KILLING IT. Copyright © 2016 by Sheryl O'Loughlin LLC. All rights reserved. Printed in the United States of America. No part of this book may be used or reproduced in any manner whatsoever without written permission except in the case of brief quotations embodied in critical articles and reviews. For information, address HarperCollins Publishers, 195 Broadway, New York, NY 10007.

HarperCollins books may be purchased for educational, business, or sales promotional use. For information, please email the Special Markets Department at SPsales@harpercollins.com.

FIRST EDITION

Designed by Fritz Metsch

Library of Congress Cataloging-in-Publication Data has been applied for.

ISBN 978-0-06-247534-3

16 17 18 19 20   RRD   10 9 8 7 6 5 4 3 2 1

To my three guys: My love for you is bigger than the universe.

And to the entrepreneurs—you all inspire me with your bravery. Know that I'm watching in amazement as you change the world!

CONTENTS

PART II: DOING THE WORK

Entrepreneurship Is a Calling, Not a Job

Since flickering torches illuminated the first people who drew on cave walls, there has always been a group of talented individuals whom we call artists. For thousands of years we've recognized that while everyone can learn how to paint, sculpt, compose, and write, there is a subset of those who live their lives obsessed with their art.

Artists suffer through failure and hardships, a perpetual lack of funding, and the derision of others who tell them "to get a real job," and they are mostly ignored by those who are comfortable with the status quo. But they push on because they see or hear something that others do not. And their passion for bringing that thing into the world drives them through obstacles long past the point at which someone just wanting a job would have given up.

To those artists, *their profession is not a job, it's a calling.* These artists feel that they have something inside them that they need to express. And they need to share it with others.

Founders fit the definition of an artist: *They see something no one else does. Their passion drives them to create something others don't yet see. And their passion drives them through obstacles that would stop others who were just doing a job.*

Startup founders bring an artist's passion and obsession but realize they need to recruit a team to make it a reality. And much like composers recruiting an orchestra, or playwrights hiring a director and actors, *they surround themselves with world-class performers.* This concept of creating something that few others see—and the reality-distortion field necessary to recruit a team to build it—is at the heart of what startup founders do. It requires very different skills than being a solo performer or a scientist at a lab bench, or being a manager in an existing company.

Employees who join an entrepreneurial startup early are the talented performers who hear the siren song of a founder's vision. Joining a startup while it is still searching for a business model, they, too, see the promise of what can be and join the founder to bring the vision to life.

Founders then put in play every skill and ability that makes them unique—tenacity, passion, agility, rapid pivots, curiosity, learning and discovery, improvisation, the ability to bring order out of chaos, resilience, leadership, a reality-distortion field, and a relentless focus on execution—to lead the unyielding process of refining their vision and making it a reality.

Both founders and entrepreneurial employees prefer to build something from the ground up rather than join an existing company. Like jazz musicians or improv actors, they prefer to operate in a chaotic environment with multiple unknowns. They sense the general direction they're headed in, and they're okay with uncertainty and surprises, using the tools at hand and their instinct to achieve their vision. These types of people are rare, unique, and crazy. They're artists.

Now that anyone can start a software company on his or her laptop and the Lean Startup has given us a repeatable way of building new ventures, entrepreneurship has become the assumed job-creation engine for the twenty-first-century economy. The assumption is that building early-stage ventures is a "science," one that has a set of tools, and that entrepreneurship is simply a job that anyone can do using these new tools.

When page-layout programs first came out with the Macintosh, everyone thought, "Now everyone can do design," and that it was going to be the end of graphic artists and designers. Users quickly learned how hard it is do design well (yes, it is an art) and again hired professionals. The same thing happened with the first word processors. We didn't get more or better authors. Instead we ended up with poorly written documents that looked like ransom notes. What we now understand is that *tools do not make the artist* (or the founder).

Artists' lives are a constant struggle with their obsession of creation. This struggle takes a toll on their relationships and their health. And after decades of toil, the result is *most artists fail.*

Yet even knowing all of this up front, most artists and entrepreneurs, given a choice, would opt to do it again—but next time hopefully healthier and happier. And that's the goal of this book, to acknowledge that the culture of entrepreneurs, just like that of artists, has the same serious drawbacks for its participants' health and relationships.

We can't make the drive for creation less obsessive, we

can't guarantee that the journey will end more successfully, but if we talk up front and honestly about the trials and tribulations of founders, we can end up with healthier teams and companies.

Sheryl has the battle scars to tell this story from a founder's perspective. Reading this book will help entrepreneurs prepare for a healthy journey that maximizes their joys and minimizes the hardships and heartaches that come with this all-consuming calling.

—STEVE BLANK

Killing It

The Light and the Dark

My day may sound familiar to you, or maybe it's the kind of day you're anticipating once you start your business. I'm the CEO of REBBL, a growing beverage company with a social and a health mission. We're a pretty small company right now; we have seven employees, and many of us work remotely. Consumers are starting to take notice of REBBL, though. I know this because I began my day today by looking at the monthly sales data and marveling at the steep climb we've accomplished over the past twelve weeks. In the last two months, I've heard many more consumers say, "REBBL? I *love* REBBL." It still astonishes me every time I realize that people actually know our product. It seems like we're hitting an early-stage tipping point.

Breaking me out of my good-news glow comes a call from our VP of operations, Librado. "Sheryl, it looks like we might not make our second-quarter margin," he says in his calm, measured tone—the same tone he maintains whether the news is bad or phenomenal. In this case, it *is* bad news. REBBL's brand might be trending in a great direction, but this development could cut our cash runway shorter than we'd originally planned. If we don't hit our margin, it will have a ripple effect on our cash needs and increase the urgency to fundraise, just six months after we closed our last round of financing.

"All right, let's figure out a plan," I say as calmly as I can, and we talk about what steps we'll take. We brainstorm some options to close the gap and agree to formally get the team together for open, honest, thoughtful conversation, and to prepare our course of action.

A few minutes later, Rachel, our community manager, emails me about some product inconsistencies that a few consumers have been calling and emailing about. At REBBL, we're committed to using organic, real-food ingredients, which is critical to our values but can be challenging to our consistency from bottle to bottle. We have to keep innovating so that we can get the predictability consumers want without sacrificing our standards. My conversation with Rachel underscores the need to solve this quickly. As soon as I hang up with Rachel, I'm on the phone with Palo, our chief innovation officer, to see if we can speed up our work to address the issue.

As I talk to Palo, a text comes through from Mike, our director of sales, to tell me that we've secured a new retail account, our first mainstream supermarket account. "Awesome," I text back, "keep up the great work." Librado then calls back to tell me one of our copackers won't be able to meet our production schedule. We need product in a month, but they can't run us until six months out! Our team is pushing back hard, but to no avail. Librado and I discuss an alternative approach.

As my next call is about to come in, my son Gavin runs into

my home office to explain that his buddy has dropped out of the state history competition they were doing together and he has only two weeks to finish it on his own. He needs me and his dad to work some late nights with him to help him make it happen. "Okay, bud, we'll help to make it happen as long as you lead the way." I take a deep, cleansing breath.

A couple of hours later, I finish my day, turn my computer off, run downstairs to set the table, and make sure Gavin has fed the bunnies and that Connor, my fifteen-year-old, has finished his homework. My husband, Patrick, comes in and we turn on some mellow jazz tunes as we sit down for dinner as a family. No big deal, no red-letter day. REBBL and I will live to see tomorrow; we'll work through the problems somehow. In the end, it's just a normal Wednesday.

Five years ago, when I was CEO of Nest Collective—which became Plum, Inc.—I would have bemoaned every piece of bad news that came on a given day. I would have hooted and yippee'd at every piece of good news. I would have come home exhausted but exhilarated. If I'd had the discipline to turn off my phone and refrain from checking my email (which wasn't likely), I'd still have obsessed over everything that had happened, replaying it over and over in my head, and strategized over how to respond the next day.

We entrepreneurs tend to be a bit intense. We're like the people who love to bungee jump and skydive, who love the thrill of being alive—only we find it in business. We get our kicks in the chase for investors, for customers, for the most talented people to recruit. My intensity is a quality that I've learned to love about myself, because it drives me forward. But here's the thing about intensity: little by little, inch by inch, if not kept in check, it turns into obsession. Unlike intensity, which stretches us beyond what may seem possible, obsession quickly becomes maladaptive. It's the difference between having the grit to stay at it for one more hour and the inability to say "that's enough for now" when you're exhausted. It's the difference between caring deeply about everything you do and caring *so much* about what you do that it becomes who you are. Intensity and obsession are two sides of the same coin, and entrepreneurs are particularly susceptible to confusing the two.

Many messages about entrepreneurship make it seem as though starting a company is all glory: an exhilarating climb up the mountain, with a big monetary payout at the peak. And make no mistake, there is glory. The feeling of being in line behind someone at a supermarket and seeing her purchase the product you've worked your ass off to produce is indescribable. The feeling of seeing your company's name twittering in social media, or catching a reference to what you're doing in the newspaper or on television, can give a rush similar to the one you get from breathing in high-altitude mountain air after a long climb. You get an enormous sense of gratitude when people look to you to lead them to an aspirational future. You get a high from making a contribution, from doing meaningful work, and from the knowledge that an idea that came from your brain is thriving in the world.

We hear stories about victorious climbs all the time. What we don't hear are stories about the day-to-day process and the difficulty of the journey, and about the rarity of actually making it to the top. Those stories don't make for sexy headlines. The profession is filled with deeply distressed or, at the very least, chronically unhappy and unhealthy people. And that discontent comes home and affects everyone else who lives there. Personal and professional dissatisfaction among entrepreneurs is not limited to Silicon Valley, or even to the United States. It's prevalent throughout the world, from Europe to India, and it's starting to grow quickly in places like Kenya.

One seemingly normal day in January 2013, I called my friend Will Rosenzweig, cofounder of the Republic of Tea and now the dean of the Food Business School at the Culinary Institute of America. We'd barely exchanged pleasantries when he told me that just days before, two entrepreneurs had committed suicide. One of these was a new business relationship of Nest's, a guy who was known to be pretty tough. I was surprised that I hadn't heard the news already, nor had I heard this entrepreneur had been suffering. But I shouldn't have been surprised—one of our great gifts as entrepreneurs is hiding hardship behind images of being in total control, of having all the answers, of the certainty that we and all those who work for us will become multimillionaires or more.

If you listen closely in Silicon Valley, you can start to hear new murmurings about failure, depression, and the growing problem of drug abuse among the valley's most intense. The conversation has focused most recently on the effect of a culture that values achievement above all else in its offspring; the ten-year suicide rate for two Palo Alto–area high schools is between four and five times the national average. As the *Atlantic*'s Hanna Rosin reported, school counselors are "overwhelmed and overloaded" with an influx of kids considered high risk. Martha Cabot, a high school sophomore, was moved to post a YouTube video message to parents after the suicide of a classmate: "We'll do just fine, even though we got a B-minus on that chem test," she said.

Rosin writes, "There, from one of their own kids, was the rebuke that in this community, no place or time or language existed that allowed kids to be vulnerable, much less broken, or even just to be: 'We love our moms and we love our dads,' Martha said. 'But *calm down.*'"

That conversation about failure, and about calming down, needs to come forward and become a real, nuanced dialogue, not only about the messages we're sending our kids surrounding their self-worth, but also about the ways we're valuing our own.

I've learned much of what I share in this book the hard way. I had great traditional "successes" as the CEO of Clif Bar and a cofounder of Plum. But the journey was at times much more brutal than it needed to be. I immersed myself body and soul in Nest, a company that was created to support independent brands, and that evolved to focus on nourishing children. The workdays were often exhilarating, including such moments as when our first investor believed in us enough to hand us a check, encouraging us to go for it when we were only just a concept with no revenue; the minute we saw our product actually come off the line in the manufacturing plant; the days that brought the signing of a new retail account; and, most important, the first time we watched a mom lovingly give our food to the outreached hand of her hungry baby.

But there were also the pressures of a seemingly endless stream of gut-wrenching decisions: Should we discontinue the line of frozen baby food that was the staple of the small company we acquired? Should we merge with one of our partner companies? Should we acquire a company in the United Kingdom also named Plum, which had blocked us from owning the international trademark for our brand? Should we fire an employee who had a lot of heart but who didn't have the skill set that his job required at our new stage of growth? Should we accept funding from an investor with deep pockets to take us to our next stage of growth, even if he didn't care about Plum's impact on people and the planet as much as we did? Would we ever want to sell the company, knowing that we would risk losing our company's soul if we chose the wrong partner? Given how much a part of me the venture was, there were times when I took criticism about the company too personally. Once, after preparing for days for an important sales call, the buyer gave me only two minutes before saying smugly, "I'm out of time and not interested." It was like being punched in the gut—moments like that physically hurt. It was an exhausting ride, each day bringing questions about whether our company would live to see another day or not. The ride at Plum was super high and super low, and I rode it all—and *hard*.

In the midst of everything that was going on at Plum, my husband, Patrick, who is also an entrepreneur, had the idea for Blue Sky. It would be an indoor play space where families could come, no matter the weather, to be active and eat healthy food. It would be the antidote to Chuck E. Cheese's. We would finance it ourselves, so we wouldn't have pressure from investors. We would control our destiny with this family business, a place where we could bring our sons to work with us. For many reasons I go into throughout this book, Blue Sky failed, bringing with it enormous personal and familial financial stress. My days were filled with taking care of my kids, who were still quite young; nurturing my husband through the devastation he felt about Blue Sky; juggling fundraising, operations, and an extremely intense investor at Plum; and determining how my family was going to claw our way back to financial health. I was so blinded with stress I could barely see my hand before my face.

In time, but not soon enough, I got off the entrepreneurial roller coaster when I became the executive director of the Center for Entrepreneurial Studies at the Stanford Graduate School of Business. Then, after a couple of years, our finances back on track, Patrick and I bought a place in wine country, and I decided to take some time off. In the quiet and beautiful space of the Santa Rosa hills, I recognized I needed to deal with some of the baggage I'd been kicking behind the couch for years. Namely, in the midst of the chaos of Blue Sky and Plum, the intensity that had fueled me for so long had turned into obsession. Slowly, I had become anorexic. It wasn't something that happened quickly, but it *had* happened, and I was frighteningly far down the road. Just as slowly, and with a lot of help, love, and patience, I began to walk back toward health.

Even once I was better (note I didn't say "cured"—recovering from anorexia takes *years*), I was sure I'd never be an entrepreneur or a CEO again. I'd done it, it had been as exhilarating as it had been exhausting, and I didn't hear the call to come back.

Until I did.

Though I didn't have a traditional nine-to-five job at the time (or eight to eight, more aptly), I served on the board of REBBL. The more I drank REBBL, shared it with friends, and learned about the company, the more excited about it I felt. It had a combination I'd come to recognize as golden: a passionate, creative team with the resilience needed to make a startup become valuable; a brilliant product innovator in cofounder Palo Hawken; a delicious product; and a powerful, mission-driven brand. When Palo and the board asked me to become CEO in the summer of 2015, I initially hesitated, agreeing to it only on an interim basis. Then I fell passionately in love with the people and the business, and jumped in to lead the company for the longer run. I wanted to be part of REBBL in a major way, and I was ready. My instincts to jump back in were right: I'm having the time of my life.

Now I know how to navigate the unknown in a way that doesn't make me lose sleep. I know how to remain engaged with my family, even when the fast growth of the company feels all-consuming. I know how to prioritize my friendships, and also my health. I'm not saying it's all puppies and sunshine. I have hard days—sometimes really hard days—because it's a hard job. But I'm on even ground, and the difficult moments pass without taking my well-being and self-worth with them.

Anorexia was *my* personal demon, but I've been around long enough to see other entrepreneurs deal with their own. Entrepreneurs all too often work in a stressful, isolating, and unpredictable environment that makes them vulnerable to drug abuse, suicide, depression, obesity, divorce, hypomania, and more. And while our demons look different, the circumstances that bring them out are largely the same. That's why I feel strongly that we need a new definition of entrepreneurial success. Specifically, "success" should not be about getting to the top of the mountain. We need to change our conversations, so that instead of asking each other how the growth of the business is going, we ask each other how we're doing through it all. Are we having fun? Are we honoring the values that are most important to us? Are we honoring the people who are most important to us? Are we respecting ourselves and what our bodies and hearts need to thrive? If the answer to these questions is yes, then if the business shuts its doors for good (and statistically speaking, the odds are that it will), the energy we have invested will not have been for naught. We will have succeeded in accomplishing an adventure of a lifetime.

The entrepreneurial world is a vibrant one, holding incredible promise and light. But at the same time, it has a dark side, too, just as the courageous people who populate that world do. The key is in knowing how to keep the dark at bay while letting the light lead. It's attainable, and I am proof of that. And it is so, so worth it.

Part I

GETTING READY—
WHAT YOU *REALLY* NEED
TO KNOW

So many people who become entrepreneurs aren't prepared for what it really takes. And I'm not talking about the stuff they teach in business school. I mean the questions no one tells you to ask, the things no one tells you to think about, and the ideas you don't know to think about. For instance, business school doesn't teach you why it's important to have good friends around you, or how to handle the emotional fallout when a cofounder relationship breaks apart. They don't tell you how to maneuver the tricky spots with your partner, or with your kids if you have them. Yet these things are arguably just as important—if not more so—than putting together budgets and marketing plans. And so here I offer you questions to ask of yourself and those around you, and advice I wish I'd heard before taking the leap. Make no mistake: even had I known all of this when I was starting out, I would have taken the leap anyway. But I'd probably have had a lot more fun.

Part 1

CHAPTER 1

Heart on Your Sleeve

The Entrepreneur and Love

I 've often wondered why we save words like "love" for home. Every moment—whether you're reading to your child, making dinner, or running a multimillion-dollar corporation—is an opportunity to create and express love. Love belongs in everything we do.

It wasn't until I met Gary Erickson—the cofounder and owner of Clif Bar—in 1997 that I learned that love belonged in work. Prior to meeting him, I worked in marketing for big companies where the conventional wisdom was that in order to effectively analyze a product, you had to remove yourself and your personal likes and dislikes. In other words, you had to remove your humanity. That was the only way to be objective. Gary's philosophy was the opposite. He brought his entire self to his business—his love for the outdoors and for being physically active, his commitment to the environment and to his family (when I first met with him in person, he interviewed me with his daughter in his lap), and his enthusiasm for food— particularly natural foods. At this point, "natural foods" was a new concept for me, considering that I got my start working on products like Kool-Aid. Believe it or not, there's not a whole lot that's natural in Kool-Aid. Gary encouraged everyone who worked with him to be as committed to the mission on a personal level as he was, to bring their full selves to their work.

I learned that to be entrepreneurial, you have to let the curiosity that led you as a child come back into your life. Watch a baby explore his world—what does he do? He wants to touch everything. He thinks, *Hmm, a ball. What happens if I crawl to it? What happens if I pound on it? What happens if I put it in my mouth?* He learns how the world works by watching, touching, poking, prodding, and waiting for the results of his experiments. If I could channel that pure curiosity and put it into my work, where would it lead me?

In part, it led to Luna Bar. Gary taught me that what was important to me might be important to others. I should look to my own life for inspiration. Well, as I got deeper into the world of Clif Bar, I discovered that I wanted something a little lighter, something that wouldn't have more calories than was practical for a light workout day but would still have some sweetness. More important, I wanted to create a nutrition bar that was just for women, with the hope, and the higher purpose, that it would ultimately be a source of empowerment. That concept, along with the perfect bar that Gary developed in his kitchen, led to a $70 million business in three years.

In 2000, Gary received a lucrative offer to sell his beloved company to a large strategic buyer. It was a critical crossroad. Gary turned the offer down, and instead committed Clif Bar to serving five bottom lines: sustaining our people, community, planet, business, and brands—that's how deep his love was for his company, and how strong his commitment to integrate it with his personal values. And I had the good fortune of running this company, which delivered against all five bottom lines.

My passion has been wrapped up in the natural food business for decades, but passions come in all forms, whether it's a delicious, sustainable nutrition bar, software engineering, or social media. One of the many entrepreneurs whose stories I collected for this book is Victoria Lai, who had a law degree and a prestigious government job when she cashed in her savings to start Ice Cream Jubilee. Yep, from the halls of government to ice cream. But that's where her passion lay. "Musicians think in whatever instrument they might play," she said, "and painters think visually. I see everything around me in flavors." Which begs the question: How do you see everything around *you*?

For Love or Money

Maybe you became an entrepreneur because you had a great idea, or a solution to a problem. Or maybe you wanted to make a lot of money and felt entrepreneurship was the way to do it. Or maybe you just couldn't stomach the idea of having a boss and working for someone else. Maybe you were driven by a desire to create something, to have an impact that you could shape and control. It's possible you don't really know what drives you. But if passion isn't in there somewhere, be it passion for the chase or passion for the product, you need to tread very carefully.

One of the many hats Will Rosenzweig wears is advising business school students. He told me that the last time he held office hours, he was struck by how many students didn't feel passion for their planned endeavors. "Many thought they were going to launch a business coming out of school, not necessarily to solve a problem, but the problem they were trying to solve was their own employment and livelihood," he said. "The naïveté of that really struck me."

By certain measures, around 95 percent of startups fail.° So starting a business for money is a gamble with terrible odds. (The popular book *The E-Myth* did quite a bit to dispel the romance around starting a company as a shortcut to owning a penthouse.) Without real love for the endeavor, entrepreneurs won't have the childlike curiosity or the motivation to spur them through the tough spots. It's love that will keep you up into the wee hours of the night to launch, say, a photography business, while you hold down a steady-paycheck job during the day. It's love that will give you the energy to lead rafting trips on the weekends and during vacations, in the hopes that one day you can make it your primary gig. You don't make those sacrifices of time, energy, and money without love. Why would you?

Larry Smith is an economist and an adjunct professor at the University of Waterloo who has served as a career adviser to thousands upon thousands of graduates over the past twenty years. In his experience, passion for one's work is not a luxury reserved for the fortunate, but a necessity to thrive in an increasingly competitive, fast-changing global economy. In his book *No Fears, No Excuses*, he argues, "Can you create any significant degree of credible edge without a passionate interest in the work itself? Can you imagine

°Deborah Gage, "The Venture Capital Secret: 3 Out of 4 Start-Ups Fail," *Wall Street Journal*, September 20, 2012.

creating this edge, this commanding competitive advantage that will survive your working life, *without* such passion?"* If someone is passionate about math, for instance, she won't merely think about numbers sometimes; math will be the framework within which she thinks about almost everything. Those who simply are okay in math or even just *like* it can't compete.

Lack of love accounts in no small measure for why so many ventures fail. Starting and growing a company is so all-consuming and takes such herculean effort that without a wild, passionate love to start with and an ongoing, endearing love thereafter, the entrepreneur will quit. It just becomes too hard. Many marriages fall apart for this reason; it only makes sense that startups would as well. What's to keep it all going, if not love for the business? Note I didn't say love for how the company serves your sense of self, or for how it makes you happy. It's a different feeling. When you love the business purely, you'll do whatever is right to keep it viable and sustainable without thought about your ego.

Love for the Solution

Perhaps love of the field or product *is* your primary driver. Or perhaps you've worked in a field for a long time, and you see a problem that you feel drawn to solve. *Why has no one fixed this, when the solution is so obvious?* you wonder. You don't just see a solution; you feel a driving need to implement that solution.

*Larry Smith, *No Fears, No Excuses* (New York: Houghton Mifflin Harcourt, 2016).

When Neil Grimmer and I came together to start a business, we used our passion for healthy, sustainable products as a launching point. We were witnessing authentic-to-the-core organic and natural brands such as PowerBar, Balance Bar, Ben and Jerry's, and the Body Shop "sell out" to mega-conglomerates in order to grow. Each of these once special brands would usually lose their soul in the process of going corporate. A few stayed independent, like Clif Bar and Organic Valley, but they were the exception to the rule. Our idea was that soulful brands would "sell into" our company, which we called the Nest Collective; we would nurture them to thrive in their financials but also in their spirit and heart. We were determined to find a way to keep Nest dedicated to this mission and wanted to find a way to get our investors liquidity down the road, without having to sell out Nest. When we first developed the concept, our idea was broad. We would acquire brands that were focused on products that you put on your body (like lotions), in your body (food or beverage), or outside your body (home care). We would grow these brands through fast-to-market innovation, user-focused design, and exceptional branding. Neil and I passionately wanted to build a company with a very special culture. We had both seen how Clif Bar was able to attract great people, retain them, and inspire them to do their best work because it was such a fun place to work, a place where you looked around at your colleagues and felt you'd found your tribe, that you belonged. It was 2007; the importance of a company's culture wasn't universally acknowledged then the way it is now. We wanted our employees to love coming to work each day, to love the mission, to love being together in our Nest family. We referred to our mission as "nurturing the human spirit." We wanted people to feel that they had huge impact in shaping our company and that each one of them mattered. We wanted to make sure that we all recognized the humanity of each other and that we never got lost in the machine of business. We would nurture Nest and each other.

In the first three months of the company, we pivoted our far-reaching idea and thought it was important to focus on a specific consumer category so that we would become experts in it. To figure out where to focus, we looked to our own lives. Neil and I were both parents of young kids, and we talked about them all the time. Neil and I and our spouses had all experienced the frustration of trying to pack a healthy lunch for our children, only to have it come home as a ball of uneaten mush. As we thought more about it, a focus on nurturing and nourishing kids fit perfectly with the idea of Nest.

The more we talked to other parents and walked the aisles of the natural food stores in 2007, the more we realized that there seemed to be this great divide between convenient and yummy food versus healthy and organic. Kids were drawn to the junk they saw in the colorful, fun packaging in the grocery store that tasted good to their palettes. And parents were forced to either spend the time making their own baby food or lugging around jars. That point had been brought home to me when Patrick and I had taken Connor, who was then just seven months old, backpacking at Glacier National Park in 2002. We went to the Granite Park Chalet, which involved a seven-mile trek in which you had to carry your own food. We carried about fifty pounds of weight on our backs: thirty-five of Connor and fifteen pounds of baby-food jars. No wonder he was the youngest kid ever to visit the place!

The point is, there was a problem that needed solving. Neil

and I went to the 2007 Natural Products Expo East trade show (the semiannual showcase for the natural products industry) and witnessed firsthand the absence of companies addressing this market. This was also when the drumbeat was becoming louder and louder about the fact that one out of every three US kids was overweight or obese. This would be the first generation of children, in the modern day, who would die at a younger age than their parents, if the trend kept going at the current rate. With proof from the consumer, the retailer, and society that this problem had to be addressed, we became determined to be the ones to do so. Our company changed as we became more focused on kids specifically, and in time Nest's mission statement changed to acknowledge this new purpose: "nourishing kids from the highchair to the lunchbox to help kids develop a lifetime love of healthy eating." At the same time, we operationally shifted our thinking from purely acquisitions to build, partner, or buy—whatever it took to achieve our goals.

Love for the Game

With Nest, Neil and I had a deep love for our purpose. But there are also founders for whom the love isn't about the subject, the industry, or even the solution to a particular problem. Rather, they love entrepreneurship itself. Some love the effort, they love the quest, they love the energy and adrenaline of it, or there's some other component of the job they've fallen for, and hard. This is why you meet people who do it again and again, the serial entrepreneurs. The subjects of their endeavors might be vastly different, but the subject isn't the point—it's the game of it all. My friend and mentor John

Hahn started, sold, and bought back his company *seven times.* Then he started a whole new company. Why did he do this? Because of the bliss he finds in the journey. In the throes of an endeavor, he finds the flow that means he's performing at his best—he's in the zone. And that feeling alone is addictive.

Pete Vlastelica wasn't a particularly avid sports fan when he cofounded Yardbarker, a network of sports websites. But he loved the thrill of the chase. "When you're an entrepreneur, you run into this crazy darkness and have to come out of the forest somehow," he said. "It's like Joseph Campbell's hero's journey." The hero's journey, for those who need a refresher, is a template that narratives from *Star Wars* to *Trainwreck* follow. It's more complex than this, but essentially the hero is called to adventure, is helped/mentored along, faces an abyss of some sort, and is transformed.

But there are other components that Pete and many others love about entrepreneurship. Namely, Pete loves the ability to steer in the direction he wants to go. "When you're working for someone else," he said, "you're inherently following *their* path. The great thing about a startup is that you get to shape it to your liking and you get to build something that's a reflection of your perspective, not just on the economy or on an industry, but on life and what people should want to buy and what the world needs more of—a reflection of your own aesthetic and worldview."

The ability to have that level of impact has always been a huge draw for me in entrepreneurship. While large companies tend to be filled with politics, you get to bypass most of that when you're at the helm of your own ship, especially when you own most of the company. You get to spend your time solving customers' problems. You get to steer the ship where you want it to go. You get to make an impact on a daily level, and to see the fruits of that impact. I will never forget when I was in the throes of the early days of Plum, and our whole company was talking with moms in this small, sunny park in Berkeley to understand what they thought about baby food. I remember walking up to this woman pushing a baby stroller. I started asking questions about baby food, and she peeled the top of her buggy back so I could see her baby sucking on a Plum pouch. I jumped up and down. It was so satisfying. And then, just recently I was leaving, of all places, the passport office—so you can imagine my frame of mind—and saw a man on a random corner of the street holding a bottle of REBBL. I was so excited that the first thing I did when I got home was email the team and tell them about it. "Oh my god!" I wrote, "I just saw some arbitrary guy drinking a REBBL!"

"Oh yes," wrote Mike, our director of sales. "You will never forget your first REBBL sighting."

Seeing a product you've slaved over out in the world is amazing, and yet that isn't even my favorite thing about being an entrepreneur. My favorite thing is the people. Of course, there are people at every job. (Well, most, anyway.) But there's something special about people working at a startup. The people are there because they want to be a part of it—they're passionate and hungry, and the energy and commitment they have is mind-blowing. For instance, at REBBL I learned that Mike didn't want to be paid a bonus. I was incredulous. In my experience, the bonus for the sales team is always a hugely important motivator. Instead, he said, "I don't want any money going in my pocket that could go to help this company survive." I got him to accept a bonus because he so deserved it, but the commitment was stunning to me.

It's deeply satisfying to work with talented people who help turn your vision of a culture into reality. If you get the right people, they join the company with the same hunger you have. You start to see how, together, you are able to move the mountain that is your venture forward in a way that you never could have done alone. And *that* is why I love being an entrepreneur—seeing people so inspired inspires me.

So this is where it's your turn to be self-reflective. What do you love about what you do? Your industry? Do you love the thrill of the hunt? Are you so drawn to fix a problem that you can't stop thinking about it? When and where are you in flow? Do you feel your pull to entrepreneurship as a calling? Does your work have a purpose? If not, find one that you are passionate about.

The Slog: When You Transition from *Discovering* to *Building*

While there is a breed of entrepreneur who loves every phase of the process, there are many more who particularly love the development, or discovery phase. And why not? It's awesome. This is the phase in which you identify the problem you're going to solve, and test ideas about how you can best solve it. It's the "whiteboard" phase, when you're looking at a blank page and filling it in. It's creative, it's intellectual, it's thrilling. You hear lots of glory stories about this phase—this is the garage you imagine Steve Jobs and Steve Wozniak in, or the bike that Gary was on when he had his epiphany that became Clif Bar. For me, it was hours of me, Neil, and our friend David Jericoff sitting in my warm kitchen, brainstorming about how we could create a company that was a source of positive energy for people.

Also in the discovery phase, you need to hypothesize, test, and learn what works. This is the basis of the "Lean Startup" methodology, popularized in Eric Reiss's book of the same name and in the work of Steve Blank. You have to find a scalable business model. Once you've found it, you enter the next phase, the build phase.

As an entrepreneur, you won't spend all your time innovating and creating. You will not spend all your time immersed in discussing and testing your vision. You need to build it. In short, the goal of the build phase is to gain traction. You have to ensure your product can be produced and delivered. You have to acquire customers. You have to find what drives growth. And you most likely have to do all of this with limited resources. It's this build phase that catches many entrepreneurs by surprise—after so much excitement, they're shocked at how mundane it all is. Remember the Buddhist saying, "After enlightenment, the laundry." Oh, and how much laundry there is.

In the build phase, Kirsten Saenz Tobey, a cofounder of Revolution Foods, woke up and drove from Palo Alto to Oakland at three every morning in order to help load the delivery trucks that would take healthy lunches to her company's pilot schools. She had an infant at home (so she wasn't sleeping much to begin with), and she pumped breast milk while she drove. In the build phase, Will Rosenzweig would go into the Republic of Tea's office on the weekends with his family. "I had a small child at that point," he said. "He would play and we would pack boxes and ship tea. We were our own mail-order fulfillment. You just have to be willing and able to do that." In the build phase at Nest, I spent more time than I wished meeting with lawyers, negotiating with investors, doing acquisitions, and developing employee agreements. I also spent time finding new copackers that could handle a bigger scale of business, finding organic-ingredient suppliers that could handle more volume, finding more investors to fund the inventory, creating board meeting decks, and endlessly looking at the financials for every move. The work wasn't as visionary oriented, since our strategy was set. It was all about me sitting, often by myself, in front of a spreadsheet or blank PowerPoint template. There was no whiteboard, no exciting debates with my favorite people about what we could do to change the world. It wasn't that sexy. Much of it wasn't intellectually demanding.

Understand that the journey will ask you to really stretch and extend your definition of the word "love." It's like raising kids: it involves the exultation of seeing them thrive in a new experience, but it also involves the tedium of endless diaper changing. And as an infant grows into a toddler who grows into a child, becoming more self-sufficient with every step, you likewise get to step back from your business as it begins to stand on its own two feet. You don't love it any less, but the intensity that was once so wrapped up in the effort subsides.

So if you love your endeavor but hate management or sweeping the floors, be forewarned: at times when there is no one else, you have to turn off the lights at night, you have to manage the daily grind, you have to write the checks. And if you don't know how to do certain things like delving deep in the finances, setting priorities, and saying no, it's your obligation to figure them out.

I love the way Victoria tested her tolerance before she took the plunge to start Ice Cream Jubilee. She tried to get herself to hate the ice cream business. She started working on it as a side hustle, after her day job. "I wanted to see how much more I'd hate it every day. If I'm talking about ice cream in every interaction, if I'm staying on Excel or QuickBooks for hours for two straight weeks, how much do I hate it? And if I don't hate it, then good. I was *trying* to get myself to hate it. I was trying to kick the habit." Victoria reasoned, rightly, that if she hated it when the pressure hadn't really mounted, then she'd despise it when the rubber hit the road. She was testing her business model during this time, sure—but she was also testing the limits of her love. She used the slog as a test for her passion.

So, like Victoria, once you've identified your love, you have to plumb its depths. Are you prepared to wash the dishes your exhausted employees have left in the sink and to harp on them to clean up after themselves like you do with your kids? Are you prepared to learn about the things you don't know, like accounting, or IT? Are you prepared to spend a whole day navigating the difference between two health insurance plans that seem exactly the same to you? Are you prepared to spend the very next day learning everything you need to know about business insurance? Sometimes these chores caught me by surprise; I was used to having more support (even though Clif was relatively small, it was many multiples bigger than Nest). I realized, sometimes a little late, that I had to *do* it, not just manage it. But the love pushed me through. Will it push you through?

Inspire Love

It's not enough just to love your business. You have to make sure others love it, too. It's part of an entrepreneur's job to help the team connect to the company's purpose. I see this as an *active* process—not something that's done just once upon hiring, but something that's done all the time. The business has to feel personal, it has to feel meaningful to everyone involved, not just the founder. There has to be a reason people want to go to work every day. Again, that doesn't mean the purpose has to be about changing the world (although I would argue that it certainly helps), but the business has to matter to everyone. Tread carefully here, because entrepreneurs tend to be visionaries— you see the great opportunities before you, and so you assume everyone else sees them, too. This is not a given.

So how do you inspire the love?

1. **Invite people to be part of the story.** Continue to retell the story of the founding of the company and engage employees with it, no matter the size. Gary came up with the idea for Clif Bar on a 175-mile ride with his buddy that he called "the epiphany ride." Every year, he re-creates the ride, and everyone in the company is invited to either ride 175, 100, 60, or 30 miles, ending in a huge picnic.

2. **Help others find how their personal passions connect with the company's purpose.** Victoria Lai works room into the schedule for her managers to play around with ice cream flavors. At Goodreads, employees are invited to include a "What I'm reading" designation in their signature line. At Plum, we'd ask people what was meaningful to them. Some of our folks weren't driven by the fact that Plum was focused on children's nutrition—they didn't have kids. But they loved the company's focus on design, or on innovation.

3. **Immerse your team in the brand and the consumer's point of view.** To develop empathy for your consumer and how they relate

to your brand, you and your team need to live it. At Clif, we would have company camping and ski trips together because that's what our consumers did. At REBBL, Palo took us through a meditation exercise because that's what our consumers do. We also order plant-based lunches for team and board meetings to celebrate plant-based foods, since the brand is about "power from plants."

4. **Hire passionate and compassionate people.** Be clear about what you stand for and how committed you are to it from the moment you post a job description. Let applicants know you are not looking for an employee, you're looking for a tribe member.

5. **Be a leader who models love, compassion, and care.** Being a leader requires tough decisions, firing people, and making sometimes unpopular choices. However, those acts can absolutely be done with love, compassion, and care. Many companies now focus on making sure any consumer interaction ends with the consumer loving the company, even if they're contacting the company due to a bad experience with a product or service. What if we all as leaders authentically put that kind of focus on our interaction with our people? When I have to let someone go, I do my best to have the person walk away feeling valued, but I can only do it if I really care about them. Ask yourself—do you know what your people love to do with their spare time? Do you know about the people they care about in their lives? Do you know what they value, and the *why* of what they believe versus just the *what*? At Plum, one of our core values was that as a company, we would wear our hearts on our sleeves. In our early days, we designed jackets for our employees that had a heart on the sleeve. The idea was that

we wanted to nurture the human spirit, because business is personal and human. People bought into that vision, and many stayed for it.

All of these practices can serve as great guidelines. Ask yourself if your team shares your love—and if they don't, why do they keep showing up for work? What do they love about what they do?

But if nothing else, don't underestimate the value of a solid, meaningful hug to remind people why they continue to show up. If you dismiss this *(Please, Sheryl! Only Californians do that!)* then you are losing an important opportunity. Consider this: I love what I do at REBBL. It is in many ways my dream job, where I am inspired by my colleagues and the mission we're dedicated to. Even with all of this inspiration, there are periods that are just plain *hard*. Right before the holidays one year, I was at a breaking point with the stress of a fundraise I was trying to close. I was trying to hold it together, to appear strong for our board and new investors. I walked into the REBBL offices and saw Palo, the cofounder, first thing. We always hug hello, but this time I just lost it and started tearing up. He could hear it in my voice and he just hugged me, harder, for three straight minutes. I could feel my tension melt away and experienced deep gratitude. It just grounded me again on what was important—the love of the team and the brand. That is the power of love in business.

Caution and Love

You've heard me preach the business gospel throughout this chapter so far: Love is the answer. "All you need is love!" Now it's time for the "but." As anyone who has ever had an ill-fated romantic relationship knows, love needs to be tempered so that it isn't blind.

If you are too in love with your business idea, you risk becoming blind to problems. A good test is to ask yourself how much research you've done on the idea's viability. Have you pressure-tested it? Have you talked to many potential customers for your product? Have you identified every weakness? Have you interviewed industry experts about it and been open to critical feedback? (Similarly, if you are too in love with your people, you become blind to potential employee issues that need to be taken care of for the sake of the rest of your people. This happens all the time.) Passionate entrepreneurs are particularly vulnerable to having visions that are too narrow, too exact. And they become like a dog with a bone—it has to be this exact vision or nothing. They get themselves into trouble because they don't listen to what the market is telling them.

An entrepreneur has to adapt, to pivot along the way—you simply don't and can't know enough when you first start out not to need to make adjustments. Your vision has to be bigger than just the four tent poles you put up initially. Stay true to your vision, yes, but do so in a way that says "How do I do this in a way that adapts to what's needed out there?" That's what happened with Nest. We planted our poles—we stated what was important to us, what our vision was (to help companies that nurtured what went in, on, and outside the body), and we went for it. Neil and I played with that vision and built a beautiful presentation about our big and broad company. And then we realized that it was *too* broad. We forced ourselves to focus, and we thought about the brands in the world that we really loved, the ones we kept coming back to and talking about. *Why* did we love those brands so much? It was through asking these questions that we realized that it all came back to our kids, and to our belief that parents needed easy ways to feed their kids healthy food. So Nest evolved to be a landing place for companies who shared that belief.

But we weren't done. One of the brands Neil and I loved most was Plum Organics, a small baby-food company founded by Gigi Chang. Plum had enormous potential, but struggled with its products and company infrastructure. When Plum joined the Nest Collective, it was clear that with the resources we could give it, Plum could be a star. We reinvented the Plum brand and the baby-food category with the introduction of the spouted pouch. Then, when we realized the potential, we pivoted again, the Nest Collective effectively *became* Plum. If we'd been too in love with our initial idea, we would never have had the success we found. Our mission still lives—and whenever I see a Plum product I think, *We did it. We fulfilled our vision—we're nourishing kids.*

When love blinds, when love narrows thinking, the inability of a venture to get off the ground is one of the more minor consequences. A great cautionary tale of blind love is that of Elizabeth Holmes, who founded Theranos. Elizabeth dropped out of Stanford in her sophomore year when she envisioned a new way of testing blood—one that would require just a pinprick, just a drop of blood, to be able to run thirty medical tests. Imagine the potential! Theranos would make screening for illness cheaper and easier. The company would change the world, obliterating epidemics one pinprick at a time. Elizabeth was a media darling, the heroine of Silicon Valley. But then an October 2015 investigation in the *Wall Street Journal* cast doubt on whether the technology even worked. Importantly, no one from outside the company has ever verified its efficacy. At the time of this writing, Theranos is under investigation from the Securities and Exchange Commission and federal prosecutors, and regulators have barred Elizabeth Holmes from running the company for a period of two years.

According to the *New York Times*, "Ms. Holmes said that she needed secrecy to keep others from stealing her ideas, but several former employees say that Ms. Holmes's steely focus on her mission—an attribute deeply admired by outsiders—made it difficult for her to acknowledge any serious shortcomings in the company's products. They say she would become angry and sometimes fire people who pointed out problems. She often spoke as though the company's technology already existed, they said, rather than as if it were still in development."[*]

At the end of the day, successful entrepreneurs are the ones who can oscillate from the vision to the execution. "One of the things I'm always trying to teach is this creative-tension model—that binds vision to reality," said Will Rosenzweig. I couldn't agree more with this. I call this "living in the tension." Most of the time, we think of tension as a bad thing. But in the tension of two opposing concepts is where you find the most creative, effective solutions. Know where you want to go with your business, love where you want to go—but let reality in.

[*]Abelson Reed and Julie Creswell, "Theranos Founder Faces a Test of Technology, and Reputation," *New York Times*, December 19, 2015.

You Don't Have to Love Every Moment . . .
But You Do Have to Love Enough of Them

Victoria Lai couldn't kick her love for making ice cream, and her store, Ice Cream Jubilee, has only grown in popularity and accolades. She still loves it—she loves the ice cream, she loves the people she employs, and she loves the greater role she plays in bringing people together to share an experience. And still there is the slog. "This past weekend I had to be at an outdoor event," she said. "I'd gone the previous year and it had been 42 degrees and breezy, and I had to stand outside for seven or nine hours selling ice cream, and it was punishing. I wasn't looking forward to it. But then I have to remember that everybody in their dream jobs has days they don't want to go to work." Even when there are hard days, and even when there are problems, she's okay with it because she sees them as *real* problems. "They aren't fabricated," she said, contrasting it with business jobs she's had where the problem is that someone won't disclose everything they know because of a power trip, or some other political nonsense. "If we have a crisis," she said, "it's because we're running out of ice cream because our line is too long, or no one's leaving even though the store closed half an hour ago. At those points, everybody is tired but we understand that everything's going well."

To my surprise, I spent most of my time at Plum raising money. I was open to learning about this area—which I knew nothing about—and I did enjoy selling the vision at first, in a time when anything was possible. But mainly what kept me going through that period was the love for our purpose and culture. I loved our kids' food. I loved walking up the stairs every morning to the sun-soaked large room where we all worked. I loved the parents and kids who enjoyed our food. I loved the people. I loved my cofounder, Neil. It felt so right when I was in the presence of our eclectic group. It was okay that I didn't love everything—I loved enough.

Yet there is a big difference between having days and even a few weeks when you don't feel like going to work, and months and years where you don't feel like going to work. If the love and excitement for what you do has been MIA for a while, it might not be coming back. And then, my friends, you know that it's time to go. Everything in this chapter points to why that's true: Because you won't be good at it anymore. Because everyone around you will feel your loss of enthusiasm, and it will hurt them. But most important, because life is too short not to do what you love. I've said it before and I'll say it again: love belongs in *everything* we do.

CHAPTER 2

The Other Marriage

The Entrepreneur and Partnership

W hen I left Clif Bar after ten years to have a new adventure, after taking some much-needed downtime, I was ready for the next thing. I didn't know what that thing was yet, but I knew I wanted Neil Grimmer to go in on it with me. Patrick had worked with him and had introduced us, and I was drawn to him immediately. Neil had worked at Ideo, the world-famous firm that developed the design thinking process that's changed the worlds of technology, consumer products, and science. Neil's ability to creatively problem-solve through *process* was like watching a virtuoso conductor coax Mozart from the newest of musicians. I saw his raw talent and had created a job for him at Clif, where we found that we had great chemistry. A tall, athletic hipster who'd gotten his master of fine arts; an ambitious, creative thinker with boundless energy, Neil was the yin to my yang. Where I'd think about the next strategic play for Clif Bar, he'd come up with a genius way to get there. I'd say, "We need a new product for our sports specialty sales channel to demonstrate our loyalty to those accounts." Two days later, he'd show me three distinctive ideas with fully fleshed out, compelling marketing campaigns. Our skills and approach to business were a perfect match.

We both loved everything about food, from eating it to thinking about its social and environmental implications. We had great conversations about everything from the best foodie joints in Berkeley to how to make the food system better. When we were together, I had better ideas. I thought bigger. Sometimes I felt as if my mind would explode because I couldn't get my thoughts out of my mouth fast enough when I was around Neil. With him, my job was pure joy.

Neil described our connection the same way. When we worked on something together, he said, "time was slowed down a little. We were more effective. It felt electric."

When I started gearing up for my post–Clif Bar endeavor, Neil wasn't working at Clif anymore, either, so he and our other former colleague and friend David would come over to my house in Oakland. We'd sit in front of a blank white flip chart and dream about what kind of business we wanted to start. We'd cram around the table in my warm yellow kitchen and riff off each other's ideas.

One early spring morning, my friend Christine Carter, a sociologist and an expert on happiness, and my friend Marissa, who'd started and sold her public relations business, joined the idea party. It was strange and completely awesome, this assorted group of people coming together to brainstorm. And we fed off our confidence in one another.

I knew I wanted to create some sort of business that would nurture the human spirit. Tapping my fingers on the oak table, I asked, "How can we work in a company that encourages people to think about goodness, about their positive impact?"

"What about creating cards with messages of positivity on them?" Christine said.

"What about a *collective* of brands doing good?" said Neil.

Marissa pushed us to think of how we'd explain our ideas to the media so we'd have a clear and compelling vision. We poked holes in ideas and dreamed up new ones. We laughed all day long. The others went home eventually, but Neil and I remained. That day and for months that followed, we went running through the Oakland Hills and talked endlessly about ideas (we obviously weren't running that fast).

Neil and I went through so much together. As our dream of Plum became a reality, he was the only person who felt the same elation when Toys 'R' Us called us to place its order; and the devastation when investors who had met with us multiple times suddenly gave us radio silence. Neil and I would laugh (the better alternative to crying) that we had sharks swimming around us, people who shared advice and much-needed resources with us, but who had open or hidden conflicts of interest. The sharks were constantly trying to find a way to get us, so we just had to hold on tight to each other on our little startup island. This wasn't just partnership—it was family.

Early on in our adventure, Neil and I traveled to a trade show and took a Southwest Airlines flight home. I squeezed into the tiny bathroom and looked down, and sitting on the floor—covered partially by the mat that sat under the toilet— was this dirty, sticky penny. I triumphantly picked it up and ran back to Neil to show him our lucky penny. He was still teasing me about pulling this disgusting, germ-infested penny from the grimy floor as we walked out of the airport. The first sight to greet us outside the baggage claim was a huge, beautiful rainbow that reached from one end of the horizon to the other.

"See?" I said. "It's a sign. Our startup will be pennies and rainbows." Given the overwhelming evidence before us, Neil had to agree.

Cofounder relationships are often close like this—they're more like marriages than business relationships. You might even spend more time with your business partner(s) than your own family. But here's where it's different: like me and Neil, most cofounders split up (Jobs and Wozniak, Allen and Gates, the examples are endless). Or if the cofounders stay involved, their roles invariably change and evolve as the business grows. The change, as I experienced firsthand, can be devastating. At the time of my split from Neil, I didn't see it as a normal part of the company's growth. It felt like a failure and not like the natural progression it was. Instead of appreciating what we'd built together, I kept going over where we'd gone wrong.

Though every cofounder relationship is different, my experience with Neil is also pretty unexceptional. In the rest of this chapter, I use what I learned to outline a map through partnership for you. I tell you what questions you need to ask to make the map clear, where the unexpected gullies and valleys lie, and where you can find the closest, sturdiest bridge to cross them.

In the Beginning: Choosing a Cofounder—or Not

When I was at Stanford, students would often ask me if they had to have a cofounder. I always said no, it's not a given but a choice. There is a beauty in taking the journey with the right partner—someone who can share the happiness and the pain at a deep level. It's also important to have someone (or several people) who can round out your experience and skills. But that doesn't mean you need a *cofounder*, precisely—it means you need close business relationships. In other words, if you don't choose to go the cofounder route, find people who can fill the holes. Not only will it serve you well, but if yours is a business with investors, a strong leadership team will help them to see that you are aware of your strengths and limitations, and that you have a desire to have the best team possible surrounding you.

As I started pondering my post–Clif Bar move, I did some soul-searching about how I work best, and I asked questions everyone should ask before deciding whether to go solo or team up with a cofounder. So if you find yourself in the space of setting up your next adventure, here are some questions to get you started:

- Do you have trouble sharing or ceding control?
- Do you work best alone or with another?
- What brings out your best self and ideas?
- What helps you when you're stuck?
- Does corroboration with other people help you move forward, or is it easier for you to move forward based largely on your own instinct?

For my part, I knew I needed and wanted a cofounder. I'm at heart a collaborator. I thrive on being in relationship with other business brains. But many people do their best thinking in solitude. Patrick is one of these thinkers. He much prefers to work alone at first, and then to surround himself with great people when he's ready. A lot of my colleagues at REBBL operate this way, too. Although I want to talk out most things right away to get to the best solution, they need time to process, and they usually come back with an even better idea. The point is, understand who you are and how having a cofounder (or not) will mesh with that.

There's also the consideration of how quickly you want to grow. Noam Wasserman, a professor at the Harvard Business School and the author of the breakthrough book *The Founder's Dilemmas*, talks about how a core founder will add fewer cofounders if what he wants most is to keep control, but if he wants to build value quickly, that founding team will be larger. Neil and I fell into the latter camp; we wanted to create a big company that would affect a lot of kids' lives. We believed we were in a much better position to do that together along with investors from day one.

Given that it's such a personal decision, I'm always careful in my choice of words when someone asks whether to take on a cofounder. But there are three pieces of advice I offer unequivocally: (1) If you don't have expertise in the industry of your company, bring on a cofounder who does—someone who will be as invested as you are. We learned this lesson the hard way with Blue Sky. (2) Assuming that you *do* have industry expertise, don't stall an idea while waiting for Mr. or Ms. Right. And (3) Don't commit to someone too early. Don't be afraid to move forward alone—you can always bring someone on later. That's a much better course than rushing into something before you're ready, before you're sure it's the right fit.

Skills and Values

I look back on my long runs with Neil, and on our countless kitchen jam sessions, and realize how critical they were in aligning our values and the vision of what our company would be. I can't imagine any cofounders *not* having these conversations. We talked about what we wanted out of our work, and the ways we wanted to contribute to the world around us. We talked about how we thought companies should be run and our leadership philosophies. We were absolutely aligned in our mission. We wanted to build a company with a culture that honored the design process and nurtured the human spirit. We believed that culture was as important as product to the success of a team and a brand. We also had the same work ethic and great trust in what we knew the other would give of their time and energy. We were in sync, we finished each other's thoughts, and I believe this enabled us to build a company we were both deeply proud of.

Many other cofounders don't share values the way Neil and I did, and they learn this too late. One woman I spoke with, Erin, struggled mightily in this arena, in part because she took on partners too quickly. "I didn't want to do it on my own," she said. "I wanted the security of other people." She met two women she liked who had complementary skills and thought they made a good team for the staffing agency Erin wanted to launch. "I had a friend who asked if we had the same values, and I said, 'They're nice people. Why wouldn't we have the same values?'" Mainly, Erin wanted to get the business going, and she felt that the more people they had working on it, the faster they'd grow, and the more fun they'd have.

Just as a crisis will test any marriage, it will test any partnership. In 2007, the economy imploded, and Erin's friend's question about values suddenly echoed loudly.

"I've always been a people person," Erin said, "and I became even more of a people person." Highly qualified people were coming to Erin looking for placement, people who never imagined being unemployed, and her focus was on helping them. "I developed such a deep compassion for them, and it changed my personality. I was developing five new friends a week." When Erin was talking to one of her partners about her approach one day, the partner shook her head and said, "Oh god, I don't need any more friends. I'll focus on the people who can get me somewhere, but that's it."

"It was a huge moment for me," Erin said. "I couldn't have imagined not having authentic feelings for people who came through our door who met with me and needed my help." It wasn't a moment when she felt that a breakup was written on the wall, though. "I immediately knew we had value differences. But I naively thought, well, we'll work through them. She's going to understand the value of relationships. She's going to cross over and see the light." Erin's partner did not in fact cross over and see the light, and the conversation was just the first sign of a deep fissure and the eventual crumbling of the relationship.

It's a cautionary tale, to be sure. You don't have to agree with your cofounder about everything, but at the end of the day you have to have the same worldview. The fundamentals— like how to treat people, how to lead, how to engage in business in the world—have to be in sync. Erin and her partner's business *was* people, and without a similar outlook on how to treat them, their partnership was irreparable.

There comes a moment when you have to have your guard up, when you have to be self-protective and ask all the questions you really don't want to when looking at a potential partner. Does he value the same things you do? Is he an egomaniac? (Note: many entrepreneurs are, because you need such chutzpah to dare to do it in the first place.) Ask questions about his purpose—in the company and in life. What is he like as a person? What does he like to do on the weekend? How does he take breaks? *Does* he take breaks? What makes him happy or sad? Ask each other how much you each want to work, and what you'll do if you feel there's an imbalance. Decide who will do what, and talk about where you will overlap. Lay out a plan for handling disagreements. Discuss your management philosophies, your beliefs about money, and your dreams for the company's future. What are you willing to do, and what will you *not* do? Ask these questions of yourself as much as of your partner. Use hypotheticals instead of speaking in abstract terms. If possible, get an outside adviser to introduce what-if scenarios. If you come across what feel like untouchable areas, topics where you're walking on eggshells, that's a sign to watch out and pay attention. That's the area you most need to talk about, either among yourselves or with a trusted adviser. You won't want to, for the same reason you don't want to poison a romantic moment with your boyfriend by bringing up how he doesn't pull his weight with the dishes. You want to enjoy the good thing you've got going with your cofounder "romance," and it's much easier to stay in that space than bring up a point of tension, even if it seems small.

Also do due diligence on other partnerships the person has had. Look at their past collaborations and how they've ended them—what does that say about their values? You may think that's an obvious thing to check out, but remember the romantic relationship parallel: when you're in love with someone, you're not running background checks on him or her. You just want to be in the moment, you want to believe in what's possible instead of looking for every possible pothole. But don't beat yourself up about it; after all, that optimism is in and of itself a very entrepreneurial trait.

The Wall of Equity

Most cofounder relationships will find themselves running straight into a concrete wall I think of as the Wall of Equity. Some will fly over it beautifully, some will crash, some will skirt around it for a while, but it's always there. The Wall of Equity is about how you'll handle compensation, how you'll divide up equity in the company, and when and how you'll revisit it. These are hard discussions, and they can get emotional. But they must happen; fight the natural urge to bury the uncomfortable, and make the conversations open and honest. Get your beliefs about equity on the table as it pertains to cofounders, and also talk about how you'll handle it with investors and employees. If you're not aligned about whether you'll even open up equity opportunities, then you've hit the Wall before you've even begun.

As with whether or not to take on a cofounder, so much goes into dividing up equity that I can't possibly advise anyone about what the right split is. I also could spend the rest of this book talking about equity formulas, but you would be both bored and a little frustrated, because still I wouldn't be able to tell you exactly what you need to do. So, knowing that it's complicated, I will say that there are three guidelines that are always true.

First, it's critical to really understand everyone's contributions. Lay it out on paper. Note how much money you're bringing in, whether you're fundraising, whether you're a product innovator. Write down exactly what everyone will be doing for the company. How much time can you realistically give to the company? How much business will you be able to bring in? Put it all out there for everyone to see, and once you have that full picture, you can determine what feels fair. A common trap I see is that if one person has the idea for the business, that person thinks he or she should have more equity. Not so. An idea is nothing without execution. And if you've picked the right cofounder, you've chosen him based on the value that he'll bring to the table. You've probably picked him because you know that your idea can't be executed in the world without the right partnership.

Second, understand that none of us has a crystal ball into the future, and equity is a conversation that doesn't end on the day you start the company. *Don't think of it as set in stone.* It should, however, be somewhat stable. You can't change equity every year, or every time your business brings in a new big client. But seismic shifts happen, and if what you once wrote down about everyone's contributions now looks vastly different, change your equity agreement. Knowing that equity may change, set aside what's known as an option pool from the get-go—shares that belong to no one but that can be awarded as the company evolves.

Third, do a serious check-in with your values. I've been in situations in which I've looked at equity allocations and it hasn't felt fair. I knew it—I knew it in my gut, I knew it in my heart. I've both ignored that feeling and, in other cases, I've acted on that feeling. *Act on it.* Because if it's not feeling right to you, it's not feeling right to others. Get out ahead of it. It's too damn easy to kick the can down the road, but that will get you to the point where you're playing defense instead of being proactive about your vision of fairness and transparency. Kicking the can will get you to the point where you're feeling shame instead of feeling like a leader. I learned this the hard way with Neil at Plum—we didn't talk about equity to the extent we needed to, and it led to my feeling like the split we had was not fair to Neil. However, I never addressed it and it hurt our relationship.

I wanted to do things differently at REBBL. I wasn't part of REBBL's beginnings, and when I came in, I saw some equity issues straightaway. Part of what I told the board I would do as CEO was to fix any issues around equity, and that became a big priority for me, as it should be for any CEO, whether he or she has been with the company from day one or not. Fair doesn't mean equal, by the way—it means fair compensation for people's respective contributions. Sorting everything out was challenging and took up a lot of my energy at the beginning, but it was absolutely the right use of my time. A feeling of fairness is fundamental.

Discomfort surrounding equity happens all the time. Roles change. Contributions change. *Life* changes. When a company grows from one level to the next and then to the next, equity needs to remain a vital part of the conversation. Because whether you talk about the Wall or not, it's always there.

Roles in Relationship

When Neil and I started out, there was no question that I would be CEO. It was a position I'd held at Clif, and having me in that role was not only a good skills fit, but it would also be important to investors. I was a marketer who understood the importance of branding, and I had experience operating a fast-growing company past the $100 million revenue level, which is seen as a critical inflection point for a consumer food company's growth or death. Neil ended up being brilliant at running the operations of the business, but neither of us knew it at the time. His expertise was innovation and branding. We felt like we had synergy regarding the importance of branding and innovation with some skill overlap, but also skills that complemented one another. We agreed on the role split, me as CEO and him as chief innovation officer, while both of us would spiritually lead the company, as most founders do. We didn't create a plan for when and if we should revisit the subject. Neil became CEO when I left Plum, and it's become evident just how gifted a leader he is. I use this example just to show that even if you think one of you is the clear CEO at the outset, in the changing startup world, you don't really know.

Many founder relationships find that roles and responsibilities shift and change. Sometimes that change creates tension, sometimes not, but it's prudent to be aware of it. Kirsten Saenz Tobey and Kristin Groos Richmond cofounded Revolution Foods while they were still in business school together, and they had honest, thorough conversations about the roles each wanted to play at the company. Kristin was clear that she wanted to be the CEO. And Kirsten was always comfortable with that. As time passed, her feelings stayed the same, but their cofounder relationship is such that she would have brought it up to Kristin if anything changed. "Some partnerships struggle over the CEO title," Kirsten acknowledged. "Some work it out by becoming co-CEOs, sometimes there's that power struggle. We've gotten along really well because I've always respected her as CEO and that she wants that title and does a really good job of it."

Kirsten feels that Kristin has a perfect blend of CEO skills: she's charismatic, a great leader, and an astute financial manager. "Some CEOs are great who are strong in one of three of those areas," Kirsten said, "but Kris is great in all of them. And I think my skill set and my passion has always been in making sure our mission and our values and our brand are always aligned." Kirsten feels her role is unique and appreciates that Kristin has always had enormous respect for the role she's played.

The point is, map out your roles at the outset and discuss how and when you'll revisit them. Begin by talking about accountabilities in the company. Make clear that there will be responsibilities you share with your cofounder, such as company purpose, culture, and goals. For others, you will need to divide and conquer to be efficient. Lay out the key accountabilities, review each of your strengths, and decide which areas make the most sense for each of you. Also, discuss titles. Ask your cofounder if there is a title or a set of responsibilities that are important to her, and share yours.

Ideally, each of you will want different roles, just like Kirsten and Kristin experienced. But you may both want the same role, and it's critical that you know that upfront. Let's say you both want the CEO title. Okay, great job for getting that out in the open. Now break it down—write out all the responsibilities associated with that title. Also discuss the pressures that the CEO needs to absorb—mainly, being accountable for the entire company performance. Are you both ready for that?

If the answer is yes, and you both want the same responsibilities, you need to decide if you want to continue the relationship. Many will get to this point and decide it's unworkable. That's not a loss—that's in fact fantastic that it's been clarified so soon.

Some cofounders who want the same title and responsibilities don't split, though, but instead split roles, becoming co-CEOs. I don't think this normally works, because it's confusing as to who is ultimately accountable. However, if you're able to create a position in which the responsibilities are clearly separated, it *could* work. For example, Patrick works at Clorox, and they have co-COOs. Each executive has a very clear, unique set of accountabilities, and company performance is at an all-time high. It takes a lot of communication to avoid stepping on one another's toes, and though a setup like this is possible at a startup, it's particularly challenging because there is so much to do to get the company going.

Don't just discuss titles and roles, but write down the job description and the key accountabilities under each job. When you have other employees, get those down on paper as well. The more clarity you have, the more streamlined work will be. At the end of each year, if not more frequently, look at that documentation. This task becomes increasingly important as the company grows. Accountabilities will change; jobs will get bigger, yet more focused. You may each find that what you want to do for the company or what you are able to do in terms of skills and time commitment has changed. Maybe one of you has started a family and the hours have become too much. Or perhaps you were in charge of all the technology behind your company's product, but the company has outgrown your technical expertise. Having those discussions openly will allow you to understand each other's thinking and will prompt you to think about it yourself.

Couples Counseling

If you talk to couples who have been married for decades, especially if they got together very young, they often say they couldn't have predicted the challenges they'd face as a couple. If they were prescient enough to take a premarriage class, they may have gone over key issues that would probably come up, but no one really knows. Will you have a sick child or be unable to have children if you want them? Will you have financial misfortune? Will one of you get discovered at the grocery store one day and become a famous starlet? (It could happen!) You can't even really imagine who you'll *be* once you've gone through these experiences. Similarly, you can't know the obstacles you'll face as a business, let alone how your partner will respond to those obstacles. But having those what-if conversations early, examining every blemish in the rock, and *continuing* to have them can help you maneuver through the terrain.

Neil and I communicated frequently at the beginning, but then we floundered. We didn't check in with one another as much as we should have. We had discomfort around equity that we kicked under the rug. We never revisited the subject of our roles. Since I was so busy fundraising, I delegated a lot of the operations functions to Neil, or he just jumped in and took them over without my even having to ask. I appreciated his help, and only learned much later that he resented how absent I was in the details. Looking back on it, he was right to feel that way. I was used to the management of Clif Bar, where it was expected and appropriate for the CEO to delegate, to keep an intentional distance from the details. I also believed it was a great way to empower others and assure them of the trust I had in them. In a startup, though, everything needs to be held much tighter, much closer. Then little by little, you can let go. But I wish Neil would have been direct in telling me that my style wasn't working for him. I may not have agreed on every point, but at least we could have had a chance to work it out, and it would have made me a better leader.

Instead, we let resentments build until one day we started yelling at each other on the couch in the middle of Plum's workspace. I don't remember what we were fighting about, precisely, but we were both so raw, it didn't take much.

We'd been so great at communicating at the beginning, but we lost it along the way. The point is, since the nature of entrepreneurship is ever changing, you will be ever changing, too. And the only way to make sure your values remain aligned or to uncover when they aren't is to keep the conversation going.

Any worthwhile relationship takes care and feeding, a truism that is exceptionally applicable to your relationship with your cofounder. When people take trips together without anyone else present, they reconnect in meaningful ways. They remember what works so well about them. It's too easy to get swept up in the day-to-day chaos and forget that there's

this live organism that needs attention to flourish. Take retreats where the whole purpose is to catch up and reconnect
as people. It will seem like a waste of time—when there's
never enough time to get tasks done, how can you possibly
carve out a few days in a sacred place, whether it be a cabin
in the woods, someone's living room floor, or a day on the
beach, with someone you see every day? But do it. Take it
away from the office. You don't need to spend any money,
and you don't have to be best friends, but you have to respect
and trust one another. You have to maintain excellent communication through all the bumps. And nothing can facilitate
that as well as spending time together and committing to the
relationship. You must address the hard stuff, or resentments
build. If your partner is not living up to your expectations,
tell him that. It may seem obvious to you, but assume best
intentions and talk it out. Do it out of love for each other and
the company. You can't fix what is unsaid. Decide now: How
are you going to make time for one another when everything
is crazy and there's no time?

Also take five-minute retreats where you can let off steam,
tell each other you're having a rough day, or just share what
you're each prioritizing. Critically, make sure you have private
time to work through disagreements. Kirsten and Kristin are
great at this—they agreed early on that they'd talk through
any tension points together, alone, before addressing staff,
and likened it to how they've learned to parent well with their
partners in their personal lives, seeking to be "aligned but
still very real" in their interactions. If you have an open office
space, go outside to be away from others. Make sure you don't
get to the point where you end up in a shouting match. This
seems obvious, but in the heat of the moment, especially in

open office startup spaces, it happens. You just blow. Even if it's not a shouting match, your people know when you're fuming—they see it in your face and your demeanor. Be genuine by demonstrating verbally or nonverbally that you're working through challenges in a calm, centered way. All businesses have challenges, just as all relationships do. Partners who work through them well make the difference between a thriving company and a struggling one.

Libby Wagner, a poet and consultant who works with organizations to help them improve their communication and effectiveness, likes to refer to difficult conversations as "courageous conversations." "Courage has the same root as *couer*," she noted, "the French word for 'heart.' So when we need to have a courageous conversation, it's something that matters to us, it's something from the heart, it takes risk."

When you feel you're biting your lip, that tension is building, that things are being left unsaid, it's time to initiate a dialogue. Libby feels that there are actually two initial conversations that need to happen. "The very first thing is you have to go internally and have the conversation with yourself first. You need to ask 'What's not working for me? What's causing me pain and discomfort?' and then you need to ask yourself, 'What do I want instead?'" When you have sorted through these answers, then and only then are you ready to have the same conversation with your partner.

Pull yourself and your partner away from the office to talk. Then start by stating the problem as you see it, asking your partner to state the problem as he sees it. Ask yourself questions like, Why might he feel this way? Then listen to the answers and be genuinely curious—not defensive—about them. Listen to your partner's point of view with a mind to understand. Throw away preconceived notions of what she may be trying to say and use empathy and compassion as your guiding lights. "Empathy is like the golden coin," Libby said. "It's the biggest thing you can put in a trust bank, and it's the biggest de-escalator of emotion."

Most important, commit to transparency and no-bullshit. Seek guidance from a trusted third party if you need it. This adviser can be someone like a marriage counselor, who can facilitate the way through trouble spots or help you to understand if you have irreconcilable differences. Because just as a volatile marriage wreaks havoc on your kids, a volatile partnership relationship can take down a company. Don't let it.

Letting Go

When Erin recognized she had irreconcilable differences with her cofounders of her staffing company, it hit her hard. "Occasionally we all get a bit depressed," Erin said. "But for the first time in my life I didn't want to get out of bed." She was spinning, fretting, and feeling as though a spouse had been unfaithful. But then one night, she explained, "I went to sleep and dreamed these clouds parted and then there was this daylight. And then I realized, 'I need to find a way to split up from these people now. It's not going to be improved.'"

It can be incredibly painful to part ways. Perhaps there is a deep friendship at stake, and you fear losing it. Perhaps you feel a sense of failure because you couldn't find a fix. Perhaps you don't want to lose everything that was good about your working relationship, even though you can't work out the problems. You may hear and use words like "divorce," "dismantle," "breakup"—it all feels so negative, and so all you want is to hide under your covers for a while.

You may feel all of these things, and I get it. But be willing to let go of a partnership if it's not going to work. Remember that *most* cofounder relationships end in breakup. You can go on your own journey, either in or outside the company, with gratitude for the experience together. Some people feel that they can't see each other again and hold a grudge forever (which, come to think of it, is the dynamic in some families, too). But what a waste of energy, not to mention a loss of what might have continued to be a wonderful and meaningful relationship.

Let what's good for the company be your guide, not your ego, and not your attachment. In the midst of stressful and emotional disentanglement, it's hard to take the long view. So take it at the beginning. Ideally, you and your cofounders will talk at length about just such a probability at the outset, so that when the day comes, it doesn't feel unexpected but more like a normal part of business. Envision the worst-case scenario in the tactical sense and decide it's workable. That said, preparing for a breakup does not necessarily mean the entrepreneurial equivalent of getting a prenup. My friend Carlos started several businesses and has had flame-out endings to some partnerships while others have been civil. He feels the breakup that went the worst, ironically, was the one where he was the best protected. "My agreement was so good that legally I could defend myself until the cows came home," he said, "and so I didn't see that the best way forward was to shake hands and get out."

Make it so you can each walk away with something that you can feel good about. Don't assume what the other is thinking—talk about it. Keep in mind the importance of leaving a company that can last, that you can be proud of for the rest of your life, where you can feel good about your value. And, if you are the one staying in the company, make sure you reinforce the value that your partner has brought to the business and the importance of the relationship in building the company together. In other words, instead of maximizing your precise takeaway, maximize the potential of the company and your relationship. Even if it starts feeling contentious, know that you can control only how you act and whether or not you are living within your value system. Take the high road and forge your path. When you look back at the fading memory, you will be able to say you handled it in alignment with who you are.

Emotionally speaking, there's no one right way to manage the aftermath of a cofounder breakup. Understanding that it is going to be hard, and helping those near you understand it, too, is a pretty key first step. I was devastated about losing Neil as my partner in crime, the person I felt closest to other than Patrick. It really did feel like a breakup, only not one that was recognizable to most people. (In other words, my girlfriends weren't flocking to my door with gallons of ice cream and a DVD of *When Harry Met Sally*.) Splitting from a cofounder isn't like leaving colleagues at your nine-to-five job. Then again, nothing about cofounding a company is business as usual, so why should the fallout be?

Neil and I were talking about it recently (we still talk and text a lot, though we live farther apart and don't see one another as much as we'd like), and he reflected on our split the same way. "It was one of the most difficult things I had to deal with in my life," he said, "second only to my wife being diagnosed with breast cancer." He reminded me that we'd been on a mission—we'd shared a deep passion to change the world, and together we were hell-bent to get better food to kids. Then he was continuing on without me, and it was painful.

What Neil and I had wasn't romantic love, but *companionate love*. Companionate love is studied widely when it comes to our family life, but rarely when it pertains to professional life. And yet it is so important. A recent study of 3,200 employees throughout seventeen organizations found that "when employees expressed what they call companionate love toward one another, people reported greater job satisfaction, commitment, and personal accountability for work performance."[*] It was companionate love that made the ride so fun at times, and so traditionally successful—and so no wonder that I experienced its absence as a great loss, and so did he.

• • •

From where I stand now, it's easy to see that there's a lot I'd do differently. But there's also a lot that Neil and I did right. We made a great company together, for one. We ran it well, and it lives on. I'm so proud of Neil and everything he did after I left to grow the company beyond our wildest dreams. And because we had great love and affection for each other, after the bumps had passed, the friendship remained. That friendship was at the forefront of my mind when I called Neil in the summer of 2015 to tell him that I was in recovery for an eating disorder. I told him that he was one of the first to

---

[*]Sigal Barsade and Olivia A. O'Neill, "Manage Your Emotional Culture," *Harvard Business Review*, January-February 2016.

recognize it and that I would never forget it. He shared with me stories of the joys of coaching his daughter's soccer games, and the fear he felt when his wife got sick. It's having those moments to share that makes getting through the hardship worth every moment. I don't understand how people disown family members. I can't imagine disowning Neil. My love for him and appreciation for our journey together means more than any period of hardship.

In fall of 2015, four years after I had left Plum, I was invited to attend a founding faculty summit for the new Food Business School at the Culinary Institute of America in the quaint wine mecca of Saint Helena, at the top of Napa Valley. By pure coincidence, Neil also attended. I was sitting in a row directly behind Neil while we listened to speakers. I could see him do things I remembered, things I used to love, like balancing a pen between his fingers like a see-saw as he listened. Later, when we broke into discussion groups, he was in my brainstorming team, and we fell right into our old, wonderful routine, and I could still read his mind just as he could read mine. As we talked about how to create classes for the school, Neil and I both championed classes based on building culture into the fabric of a company. I could anticipate what he was going to say, and we built on everything the other said.

As I drove home from the summit, I thought about one of my favorite times with Neil—the night we went out to a fancy dinner with our spouses to celebrate Nest's one-year anniversary. We picked this elegant restaurant called Boulevard in downtown San Francisco, and we all dressed to the nines. I still remember the black-and-white dress I wore, and the high heels that were so high and slippery that I nearly had to crawl across the marble floor to use the bathroom. All four of us felt so connected about how momentous the anniversary was; the year had been hard, yet deeply fulfilling. Gone were the early days of sitting around my kitchen and jogging in the hills. We now had a cool office and deeply passionate, smart employees; we'd completed our first partnership deal; and we'd brought on more investors. At one point Neil and I were alone at the table and we just looked at each other and said, "Wow." We were full of hope and deeply proud. Years later, reflecting back on this moment didn't make me nostalgic or regretful. Rather, it simply warmed my heart.

CHAPTER 3

The Virtues of Candor

The Entrepreneur and the Supportive Tribe

I attended a bar mitzvah recently for my dear friend Allison's son, Matthew, one of the rare opportunities for me to be around other Jews. I was raised Jewish, and Patrick was raised Catholic. In raising our kids, we've focused on the values that we've found meaningful in both religions, so we haven't dedicated ourselves to one faith. I haven't spent much time in the Jewish community in years, and it's fairly rare to find Jews where we live now. The ritual of Matthew's bar mitzvah service pulled on my heartstrings, reminding me of my childhood, yet there was also a part of me that felt a bit out of place. Maybe I didn't belong, given my distance from the religion. But in the middle of the service, the rabbi stood at the bima with her powerful yet gentle voice and reminded us of what bound us all together. "Anywhere you go, anywhere in the world," she said, "you can walk in and say 'I'm a Jew,' and you are embraced as part of the tribe. You become part of it because you're Jewish, and we are bound together by our common history and experience." Her words filled me up, and I felt their truth. Surrounded by the familiar songs, prayers, and smells of the synagogue, I grasped my connection to those around me. We had a shared history, a shared experience. Tears began to well up in my eyes. I felt such a sense of being home again.

It may not be faith based, but entrepreneurs are a tribe, too. That's why whenever an entrepreneur asks for my advice, I take the time to give it to him. I *know* him; I know what he's facing. He's one of us. We need to support each other so we become stronger over time and create increasingly better businesses for the world. We're a community, and there are countless ways we can and should help one another. But far too often, for reasons that are deeply ingrained, we don't. We hide things from our peers. We're less than forthcoming about what's really going on with us. We're so committed to an exterior of calm and control that we cannot allow anyone— even others in our same circumstances—to see any cracks, even though others might be able to help us repair them if only they knew. This chapter deconstructs all the whys of our unwise ways, and charts a new way forward, so that when we meet one another we will recognize our tribe and will tear down the walls that separate us.

The Things We Don't Say

Around 2009, I met a friend of mine, Joe, for a glass of wine at a hip Chicago restaurant. We sat outside, taking in the warm evening air and watching groups of well-dressed people come and go. Joe had started a snack food company over ten years before, and we'd gotten to know each other because his company was deeply committed to sustainability principles, as was Plum. Over the years, from time to time, we'd spent a few hours together strategizing about how to source environmentally friendly packaging, and trying to top each other with who had the most frustrating encounters with a notoriously challenging buyer we had in common. He also confided to me about drama in his love life. Since I'd been married for fifteen years and had two kids, I was far removed from the dating world. I was fascinated by his stories and was happy to offer sisterly advice. But on occasion our conversations took more serious turns. One of the many things I admired about Joe was his spirituality. He was different from a lot of the other entrepreneurs I knew, in that he could transition from talking about packaging, to dating, to existential questions of life as if it were completely natural. He had cofounded his company with the same deep commitment to serving a spiritually important purpose while remaining meticulous about the quality of the little stuff.

When we met for a drink this time, though, Joe had one particular thing on his mind. "We're celebrating tonight," he said. "Drinks are on me." He was excited because an investor, Larry, had committed to investing in Joe's company. The amount of his investment would allow Joe to take his company to the next level. "He's the perfect investor for me," Joe said, and told me all of Larry's experiences working with sustainable-foods companies, and his commitment to the mission of Joe's business. "But of course," he added sheepishly, "you already know all of this."

I did. Larry had been one of my investors as well. He was an international investor with white blond hair and blue eyes. He brought a worldly perspective to the business that I appreciated. I knew how great he appeared to be and, at times, was, in terms of the values he articulated. I knew, too, the promise that all of his capital could bring to a company. But I knew more than that. Mainly, I knew that Larry was extremely challenging to work with. He was volatile, condescending, and could throw off my balance and focus by a livid call or inflammatory email (which I began to refer to as "nastygrams"). He was unreasonably demanding and could drain the energy out of a room like he was pulling the stopper out of a bathtub. He would ask tons of questions—some that were good but many that were not—and I spent more time scrambling for answers than benefiting from valuable counsel from him. Larry always advised me to never surprise him with ill-timed bad news. Yet he shocked me constantly with the bombs he'd throw my way, only to sing my praises the next day as if nothing had happened.

The first time he'd berated me—while on the phone with me and Neil—I called him back the second our call was over. "You cannot talk to me that way," I said. "It undermines me in front of my partner, and it's simply unacceptable."

"Whoa," Larry said. "Okay, Sheryl, good for you for calling me on it."

I squared my shoulders and stood a little taller when we hung up. But a month later, after he officially became our investor, he was shouting at me again. The next day, he was as calm and docile as a lamb, and then the following day he was on the warpath. I never knew which Larry would show up, and the uncertainty put me constantly on edge. During one particularly bad spell, Larry screamed at me for making a fairly minor decision without consulting him first. It was completely inappropriate for him to have been so involved with that level of operation—he needed to let me do my job. But

that didn't mean that I wasn't shaken—and literally shaking—
most of the times we got off the phone. Instead of considering
his tirade just another pebble on a long, windy path, instead
of taking a deep breath and regaining my focus, I'd replay the
conversation in my head all day, and it was still running on a
loop as my kids told me about their day at school. Then, Larry
would do something utterly surprising, like sing my praises
publicly.

Although I believe that Larry's intention was to drive top
performance, his actions ended up undermining my confidence and had me spending time and energy on things that
didn't improve the business. And, since he was an early investor who believed in us when many others had not, Neil and
I felt indebted to him. We didn't want to screw with a seemingly good thing by pushing back. It was a bad situation, plain
and simple. It wasn't something I'd wish for a friend like Joe.

I could have told Joe about my experiences with Larry. I
could have warned him what it might be like. But instead, I
raised my glass of Chardonnay and said, "Cheers! That's great
news!"

I ran into Joe a couple of months later at a trade show and
asked how it was going with Larry.

"Great!" he said. "Yeah, it's all really exciting." We talked
just a minute or so more before giving in to the crush of movement that defines trade shows. But the encounter stayed with
me. Joe had seemed genuine, his smile as easygoing as ever.
He was doing "great" with Larry. He wasn't having the problems I'd had. I was happy for him, but it felt like another mark
against me. What had gone so wrong with *me*?

About five years later, I called Joe to check in, since we
hadn't connected in a while. At this point, I'd left not only

Plum but the game altogether. I was finding my footing in the Santa Rosa countryside by then and wasn't yet working at REBBL. I was removed from everything, which is perhaps why the conversation unfolded as it did.

After five minutes of niceties, Joe's voice turned sober. "I'm having serious problems with Larry. He's completely at odds with our company culture and long-term goals."

His candor caught me off guard. "I know," I said. "I'm so sorry I didn't tell you about him. He's a nightmare."

"It's okay, Sheryl," Joe said, breathing deeply. "I know that I seemed so gung-ho about him that it was probably hard to say your truth. What's past is past. But do you have suggestions as to how to deal with it?" We talked for a while, sharing ideas about how to stay above the emotion. "Be strong with Larry," I advised. "If he's overstepping his role, tell him to back off, that he's out of line. Stay above the emotional roller coaster. Hold your boundary, and if you ever start to doubt where that boundary should be, seek help from another board member."

After a while, Joe said, "I've talked to a lot of other entrepreneurs Larry's worked with, and when I've opened up, they've *all* said the same things about him."

Though Joe didn't realize it, that comment shook me to the core. On one level, I couldn't believe he had gotten people to open up. On another, I kept thinking, *What if someone had told me? What if I'd known about Larry's reputation? Would I still have taken him on as an investor? And even if I had, would I have lost as many hours of sleep? Would I have experienced the extreme burnout I felt at the end of my journey?*

This scenario with Joe was about one investor, one difficult hurdle we'd both faced. But what lay behind it was much more significant. What if, as entrepreneurs, we didn't talk only about innocuous things like packaging struggles and difficult buyers? What if we talked about the hard stuff, too? If we created a safe, confidential, and supportive environment—a tribe—we could avoid serious mistakes. We could grow stronger. And we could enjoy ourselves more along the way.

Why We Don't Talk to Each Other

Very early in my career, I worked at General Foods on the Kool-Aid brand. I was eager and excited, and went into interactions with people assuming that everyone had good intentions, said what they meant, and meant what they said. That's what grown-ups should do, right? I may have drunk too much Kool-Aid. (Come on, sometimes even bad jokes beg to be made.) I was assigned to give a potential vendor information about a Kool-Aid program that I managed called the Kool-Aid Wacky Warehouse, a club in which kids saved labels to get free toys. From the information I provided, that vendor was to make a proposal to my boss about how working with his consulting firm would add value to our program. When the vendor gave the pitch to my boss, my boss wasn't impressed. I thought, "Okay, no big deal—we work with other vendors, and less than stellar pitches happen all the time." But the vendor felt differently. When we didn't move forward with his company, he called my boss and said, "Sheryl didn't give us good information. That's why our pitch was flat."

Well, I called bullshit. I'd given him the same exact information I gave the other vendors, all of whom had come up with better ideas. My boss backed me, and the moment passed. No big deal. But it was the first time in a business setting when I realized, *People are mean. People lie. People are ultimately out to protect themselves.* Now that I'm many years older, I see the situation differently. This vendor was most likely afraid of losing a big account, or even of losing his job. He was likely feeling desperate and was certainly feeling defensive. He was wrong to throw me under the bus, but he wasn't necessarily an evil guy. He was just a guy, and he had a story that I'll never know.

Self-protection is an instinct that runs deep in all of us, and it's ever present in business and among entrepreneurs. Everyone has a Kool-Aid story. All people have walls upon walls that they've built up. Sometimes those walls do help us. Other times they isolate us from one another, or cave in on top of us.

This deeply learned lesson of self-protection is part of what kept me from warning Joe about Larry early on. But there was more. For one, Joe wasn't asking for my opinion. It's not unlike the scenario in which your friend cooks a new recipe for you that he's excited about, but you find it salty and mushy. *He didn't ask your opinion, so eat up and shut up, Sheryl.* Also, he was celebrating. He was excited, and I didn't want to kill his buzz or suggest I questioned his judgment.

I trusted Joe, but I also had a healthy paranoia of word getting back to Larry that I'd criticized him. The entrepreneur-investor world is much smaller than you might imagine, and even people with the best intentions are prone to getting overly chatty after a few cocktails, or to filling awkward silences with whatever comes to mind. I'd been on the receiving end of many conversations in which I'd thought, "Why is this investor telling me this about so-and-so's personal life?" I knew I'd be furious if he or she shared such details about me with anyone else.

But there was another, bigger obstacle that had held me back from leveling with Joe, and it was that entrepreneurs are conditioned not to show weakness. The current conventional wisdom is that showing weakness can inhibit your bottom line if you're an entrepreneur. Weakness signals to your investors that you don't have it all under control. It signals to your employees that they should think twice before following you. It signals to your customers that perhaps they should shop around before committing to your product or service. The entire construct of the entrepreneur is to believe in the vision, sell the vision, and sell his or her ability to realize the vision. It's a role in which weakness has no place. There are many times when being tough and appearing in complete control are legitimately important, such as when you're raising capital to fund your company or when you're bringing on a new supplier that could change the trajectory of your business growth. But that's just one stage, and just one way of being. Every stage has a purpose and will require something different of you. If you still have the "everything is awesome!" song playing on a loop when you are not selling anything, if you realize that you have never turned it off, not even once, not even for a minute, stop the music. When the ever-bullish cheerleader persona is the *only* way you are as a leader in the world, it can isolate you from the help and support you inevitably will need. Further, it will damage your credibility.

All these things were at play with Joe for me. My fear of showing weakness has been around a long time. As a woman, I felt the pressure to appear strong in front of male peers like Joe particularly acutely, since there are so few women founders. Women fear that any weakness reinforces ill-conceived perceptions that we are not fit to be entrepreneurs. It was this fear of showing vulnerability that had prevented me from telling my other investors about my troubles with Larry, even when one of them gave me an opening and hinted that he recognized that Larry was a problem. It was this fear of showing weakness that had long prevented me from talking plainly and honestly with Joe.

I also felt that the problems I was having with Larry were my fault. I worried that I was taking it all too personally, that I was riding an emotional roller coaster that I could get off if I only had the gumption to do so. I was just letting it bother me too much. Larry was the loose cannon, not me, and I knew that—but why couldn't I ground him? Was it because I wasn't worthy of the role? Was it because I wasn't skilled enough to do so? His behavior was terrible, but I also felt it was *my* failure. Now I can see how utterly wrong this was. Sure, I could have done a better job keeping him at arm's length. I could have sought support. But I couldn't have changed who he was as an investor and how he treated entrepreneurs.

Why We Need to Talk to Each Other

When I was at Clif in the midst of launching Luna Bar, my mornings were occupied with thoughts of how much I needed to get done for the day. I was amped and ready to produce. I'd come from a corporate environment where you were expected to be rolling as soon as you walked in the door. Everything was about the business, and having a chat with colleagues just burned through time.

At Clif, it was different. It was about being real and human together, and creating brands that reflected our lifestyles. A smart and deep-thinking woman named Sarah, who liked being productive just as much as I did, reflected the Clif culture. Before we dug into work, she'd say, "Hello, how are you? You won't believe what happened last night . . ." and would proceed to share a funny story or occasionally vent about not being able to sleep. It took me a while before I grasped that part of my job as a leader was to welcome her doing so, and in fact to *invite* it. Those chats helped me get to know her—what made her tick, what made her happy and what pissed her off. And, equally, she wanted to really know me—what was important to me as a leader and, more crucially, as a person. Being authentic at work helped bring realness to the relationship and richness to our brands.

These conversations were about being a sounding board and a caring ear for Sarah. They were about bringing my best self to work each day, ready to absorb anything Sarah or anyone else needed to talk about. It was about helping my team to feel like they could be open with me because I cared to listen and understand.

From the moment you walk into the office, you want—and need—to feel on. But what if something is weighing on *you*, heavy as a backpack full of bricks? It could be the week's low sales numbers. It could be a volatile investor. It could be something in your personal life, or something tied up with your personal finances. You can't tell everyone what's going on—it won't help to make people anxious just because you are. But that doesn't mean the load you bear is invisible, either. When you go into the office with this backpack of bricks, you affect everyone, whether you know it or not.

Now, there are certain things you can and can't disclose to employees, and I go further into that in a bit. But even if you can't tell *them* everything, you need to tell *someone*. You need to get help and support from another entrepreneur who knows what you're going through and can help you navigate it. This will allow you not only to be in the zone when you need to be, but also to improve the culture around you.

We form friendship groups, parent groups, and bereavement groups all the time—as human beings, we understand that gathering together with like-minded people experiencing the same thing is healing and uplifting. But we don't do it nearly often enough when it comes to business. In fact, it's one of the first things to hit the cutting-room floor when you're looking at the overly packed film of your life. Who has the time? And it feels really vulnerable when you sense that you may be judged and your reputation destroyed. Make the time—it's that important.

In fact, some of the best people to talk with are your peers, those who understand what you're experiencing firsthand, but who aren't working directly with you. If you find peers you trust, there's nothing that should be off the table for discussion. Such peers can see your problem from a fresh perspective, and if they're in a different industry, it'll be easier for you to be open and share sensitive concerns. You can start finding them at networking events, or you can join a group like Vistage, Entrepreneurs' Organization (EO), or the Young Presidents' Organization (YPO).

Note that while talking with entrepreneurs outside your industry is important, so is talking to entrepreneurs *within* it. In food entrepreneurship, for example, many pressures are common with entrepreneurs in other industries, but there are many others pressures whose challenges are unique. The larger entrepreneur groups can be useful for big-picture support, but you also need someone who understands your business, who will really grasp why something is so troublesome to you, and who will offer meaningful suggestions based on his or her own knowledge.

Over nearly the past twenty years, I've been a frequent attendee of the biggest annual natural food trade show of the year, Natural Products Expo West. I missed it for three years in a row while I was focused on teaching, and I just went back in 2016. To be honest, I dreaded going. I was busy and I knew the trip would be exhausting. But it rocked. I saw people I hadn't seen in years, and it was energizing to reconnect as tribe members. I also met entrepreneurs for the first time who I knew would become important members of my tribe.

If you can't find a group like one of these, another option is to create one, in the true spirit of an entrepreneur. It's not like you have to go out and hand out flyers; just talk to people, like you're most likely doing anyway. If you click with another entrepreneur, ask if she would be interested in getting together every so often for mutual help. Ask if she'd be interested in doing it one-on-one or broadening it to involve others whom you both know and like. There's no need to formalize it or make it high maintenance, especially in the beginning. Just commit and follow through! Through that one conversation, you can start to form your own tribe. If that first connection doesn't end up working, there are plenty of others out there that will. And on the flip side, the connections that click have the potential to become meaningful friendships. I consider the people I've worked and networked with to be some of my closest friends.

When entrepreneurs don't rely on one another, they don't harness the power of possibility. Too often we approach our work from a mind-set of scarcity and not one of abundance—a mistake that holds us back. When I started business school, I remember the fifty students in my cohort all glancing at each other the first day, clearly sizing one another up: *This is my competition. We will all be competing for the same jobs.* We were not completely wrong. But, as we came to realize, those classmates were our best resources, referrals, and sounding boards. After twenty years now, when we get together telephonically, through social media, or in person, we look back and laugh at ourselves. There is more than enough work to go around, and we are all better at what we do because we challenge one another, provide sage advice, and offer contacts to each other that have been life changing for many of us. Our "competitors" have become our greatest allies.

A final reason to ask hard questions and get honest feedback from other entrepreneurs is that the decisions you make daily are incredibly important. They can have a profound impact on your destiny and the destiny of others. Why would you make such important decisions without all the information? Why wouldn't you get the help of a less invested third party, someone who can help you step out of your own head a bit and take the long view? You probably wouldn't buy a car without checking consumer reports and asking your friend who drives a similar car how he likes it. You might not even try a restaurant without asking a foodie friend if he's been and how it was. Before breaking up with a girlfriend you might ask a trusted friend if he thinks you're overreacting. The point is, we get help from our peers all the time, about decisions that are much less consequential than the decisions a founder makes. So why wouldn't you ask for help? The information is all right there, if you'll only just look.

The Great Tribeship Test

I was part of a peer-advisory group called Vistage. It has members from many different industries; the commonality is that its members are all CEOs and entrepreneurs, or they are part of "key groups" which are specifically for executives reporting to a CEO. One guy in my group ran a concrete business, another was a serial entrepreneur, and another was a CEO in the advertising business who had to change and morph constantly as the ad world did. I joked that she had as many changes of persona as Madonna. For my part, I changed a lot during my time with the group, too. It was my turn to host my group at Clif Bar the day I learned that Gary was making me the official CEO. I told them about the CEO promotion, and we all celebrated together. Then, later on, this group listened as I pondered whether I wanted to be at Clif anymore. Another time we met was when I was at my lowest, with Blue Sky falling apart. I brought Patrick to that meeting, too, wanting him to have a slice of the support that I had always gotten. This group lived through all these changes with me—they had seen me fall in and out of love, and they *got* it. They lived in the same scary entrepreneurial world I did, and they understood perfectly.

Though groups like the ones I mentioned are great starting points and may even be all you need, others of you may find that larger groups aren't for you. I tend to prefer smaller groups, and so I split off with three other women from our Vistage group, and the four of us met together regularly over the years. It was with this group that I fully realized the importance of what I call the Great Tribeship Test: *Would you cry in front of them?* If you wouldn't, then the level of support—or your ability to ask for it—isn't enough in the group, and you need to keep looking. The entrepreneurial profession requires that a person be vulnerable in order to remain healthy, and it's critical to have a space in your life with others that allows for that. Of course, if you cry every session, people may have a tough time supporting you. But have a good cry once in a while.

My Vistage subgroup included Colleen, Mary, and Deb. We became not just colleagues but also friends, people who deeply care about one another's well-being. We went through some hard stuff together, like when Deb was floored by the amount of money she was required to raise for the health care startup she led. It was an astonishingly high number, and we understood her stress. We each had moments like these, moments when we'd say things like, "I feel like everyone in the world is against me. And it's only when we talk that I feel like I'm not crazy."

My moment of greatest need with this group came when I was thinking of leaving Plum. We had a plan to meet at a restaurant in Walnut Creek, and even though it was close to my house, I was an hour late and had forgotten my wallet. I didn't even bother to hide my distress from them—not that I could have. When I walked into the restaurant, I let it all go. "I'm out of my mind," I said, breaking down and crying. "I have to be able to do something else." They talked me through it—not asking me to be anywhere else, but holding me in the desperate place I occupied. They helped me see another future. They helped me be hopeful. "Oh my gosh, what if you became a teacher or a dean, Sheryl?" they said, giving me one idea after another. "You would be able to help our next generation and how it looks at business. That would fit what inspires you so well." They helped me see that life did not have to end. They built my confidence and showed me a bridge to a possible future.

I would like to say I've had conversations that got this real with men, or that it's easy for men to access the level of intimacy my women's group got to so easily, but that's not the case. This isn't men's fault; we've all contributed to a culture where men can't easily open up. But they are the ones who lose out. The *New York Times* columnist David Brooks once wrote about the need to shed a light on how men's roles are no longer working. "There are many groups in society who have lost an empire but not yet found a role," he wrote. "Men are the largest of those groups. The traditional masculine ideal isn't working anymore. . . . This is an economy that rewards emotional connection and verbal expressiveness. Everywhere you see men imprisoned by the old reticent, stoical ideal."[*]

I have seen men be entirely vulnerable and have a good cry with a group. But I would love to help men pass the Great Tribeship Test en masse. For that to happen, men need to do several things. As David Brooks suggests, men need to chip away at the masculine ideals they unthinkingly perpetuate. So to my male readers, I say, open up to one another, and also open up to women. I saw a few men do it in my Vistage group, and the support they got was overwhelming. Or create your own group in which the Great Tribeship Test is not the exception but the rule. Take the best of what women have to offer and the best of what men have. Use this yin-yang to be powerful and compassionate, confident and open, at the same time.

[*]David Brooks, "If Not Trump, What?," *New York Times*, April 29, 2016.

The Power of *Real* Conversation

Recently I was on the phone with a woman named Marla, an ambitious entrepreneur who founded and then sold her company in the home-cleaning industry. I'd met her in the early days of Plum, when she reached out to me for advice on a growth transition with her company. Three years after I left Plum, she called me because she wanted to interview for a position there. She was looking for advice on how to sell herself and convince Plum that she was ready and willing to take a step down in title.

As she was talking with me, her voice sounded mechanical and tired. After listening for a bit, I said, "May I give you some direct advice?"

"Sure," she said. "I'd welcome it!"

"You're obviously a thoughtful professional with a great deal of experience and skills. But you'll never convince a purpose-driven company like Plum to hire you without demonstrating passion. I don't hear it in your voice, and you're not really showing how much you want this."

There was long pause before she said, "I can't believe you just said that."

I held my breath, thinking I'd really pissed her off. But then she started crying and said, "I'm so sorry. I'm sitting here with my son, who wanted to miss school today to spend the day with me. But I'm making business phone calls, and he keeps getting upset, telling me that I'm being a bad mom. He's saying I shouldn't be doing work because I don't have a job right now. But I'm a single parent—I need to work and I need to put in the time now that it takes to find a job." I reassured her that she could cry all she wanted, and then the floodgates really opened. "It's just been so hard being an entrepreneur, growing my company, and feeling like I'm never giving enough to my family. Now I'm trying to figure out what's next while I still have more pressure than ever on me, and I'm losing my confidence in every role I play in my life."

Here I was, practically a stranger, but she was in such desperate need of support that she opened up fully and completely. But I'd been there, so we had a real conversation.

What's remarkable about this conversation is how truthful we were with one another—I gave her candid feedback about her lack of energy, she gave me her candid story about what was really going on. Imagine how differently this conversation could have gone. I could have given her surface-level advice about how to impress the folks at Plum. She could have thanked me politely and moved on, without ever telling me about her reluctance or vulnerability. In other words, what a pointless exchange it would have been. Instead we got to the heart of the matter. We shared openly with one another, we learned from one another, and I believe we both took something really valuable out of the exchange. This conversation represents the great virtue of candor and the power of *real* conversation.

Jeffrey Hollander, the founder of Seventh Generation—a company that makes environmentally safe products—has been having such conversations for years. After he was fired from Seventh Generation's CEO position and dismissed from the company's board, he could have papered over all the drama in order to save face or look strong. Instead, he was open and vulnerable. "I was fired six months ago after twenty-three years," he said in a speech in 2011, "and I was never allowed to set foot back in the company."[°] He said he regrets failing to protect the company's values in the corporate structure, which would have ensured a more democratic process; he took too much money from the wrong people; he didn't give enough of the company to the employees; and he didn't create a truly sustainable brand.

These were words of warning to other entrepreneurs in the sustainable-business area. These were words that were free of self-protection and free of the jockeying for investment money or the next opportunity. He was simply honest and candid, and felt he could help some people by being truthful about his weaknesses and mistakes. Imagine if we all did this. Imagine what we could learn from one another's truths.

But perhaps the moment of truth that floored me the most came from where I'd least expected it: from Larry himself. He told me openly about how after he left as CEO from the company he founded, he'd nearly come unhinged. He had some serious personal issues and could barely function. But here's the kicker: he didn't tell me this until *the day I was leaving Plum*. Why on earth not? It would have humanized him to me. It would have helped me understand where he was coming from, and shown that he might just understand me a little bit, too. But I think he would have found it akin to showing a crack, and that was something he felt he could never do while we worked together. His finally opening up actually helped me respect him more, because I knew he'd truly experienced the ups and downs of the entrepreneurial journey.

[°]Jen Boynton, "Jeffrey Hollender Shares Four Reasons He Got Fired from Seventh Generation," *Triple Pundit*, June 9, 2011, www.triplepundit.com/2011/06/jeffrey-hollender-seventh-generation-fired.

It was that honesty that allowed me to reach out to him later for advice when I had several options in front of me. I now see Larry as a well-meaning businessman who had something to teach me. I'm a stronger leader because I've seen how losing your confidence can lead to your losing your way as a leader. I only wish Larry and I had done the hard work of being honest with each other earlier.

Whom to Talk to about What

My friend Kelly was a partner in a small law practice, which she was considering leaving because of tensions within the partner group. She had drinks one night with an assistant who worked in their office and found herself spilling some of the anger she felt toward her partners. On her way home, she regretted letting her sensitivities show so much. "Normally," she told me, "I try very hard to walk the line between being transparent—which I feel is so important and which I think my partners have traditionally sucked at—and not being confessional. But sometimes that line is hard to see." I couldn't agree more, and have offered some guidelines around this very precarious balance.

Clearly, my mantra is to open up to people. But you have to be mindful about whom you're talking to and what you're saying.

Investors and board members: You need to tread carefully here, because it's legitimate to worry about losing their confidence. You can't say, "I'm falling apart," to this group—their primary responsibility is not to you, but to the business, and it sets up an inherent conflict for them to know things that would worry them about the future of the business.

That said, your investors can and should be a valuable re-source for you, so use them as such. The best investors are not just a checkbook, but people with long and deep experience who are sounding boards, devil's advocates, and big-picture counselors all at once. I have one investor at REBBL whom I check in with every week, not because either of us requires it, but because talking things through with him helps me think better. Test the waters as you're exploring investor relation-ships; get a sense of how they think. Notice how they address issues in the boardroom or on the phone with you, and how attuned they are emotionally. Many investors and advisers want to help—they should want to help, in fact, because the stronger you are, the stronger the company will be. The best investors and advisers know that. Brad Barnhorn, a founder turned leading board member in the food and beverage in-dustry, said his personal mission is "to help CEOs build awe-some companies . . . and have an awesome experience. It's so frustrating to see a CEO build a great company and have a completely unenjoyable and unfulfilling experience of it—and it's so common."

If you are having difficulties with *other* investors or board members, you should absolutely open up about them. I could have gone to one of my investors, who was a friend and long-standing mentor to me, and said, "I need to talk to you in complete confidence about Larry. I'm having a hard time handling him and would like to do some role-playing."

I've learned these lessons. When I brought in investors at REBBL I knew much more about what they were like not just as businesspeople but as "people people." I sought inves-tors who have a spirit of partnership, including being calm and willing to help in any way. And it worked. As I struggled with a difficult business relationship recently, I went to other REBBL investors to ask for help, and they were thoughtful and smart in how they helped me navigate the situation.

Partners: I shared almost everything with Neil, and I don't regret it. All I regret is not doing it consistently until the end. If you have chosen the right partner, you should be able to be candid without fear of repercussions. If things go south, you may regret being so open, but it's far better to prevent things from going south in the first place by sharing all.

Employees: Again, not everything is appropriate to share with the people who work for you. To some extent, it's your job to shield them from the daily bumps the company experiences—you absorb those jolts so they can do their job. Mark Suster, a former entrepreneur and the author of the article "Entrepreneurshit," wrote,

> Early on in my first company I had an employee ask if it was a good time to buy a home. We had less than six months' cash in the bank. I was *pretty sure* we were going to raise another round of capital. But not *sure, sure*. I mean you never know if your investors are REALLY going to keep backing you. And you can't go around telling all your employees your deepest insecurities about it, or you'll soon have no more of said employees.[*]

Not only that, you may be wrong. What if your nervousness causes them to leave, only to then have the funding come in

---

[*]Mark Suster, "Entrepreneurshit. The Blog Post on What It's Really Like," *Both Sides*, November 18, 2012, https://bothsidesofthetable.com/entrepreneurshit -the-blog-post-on-what-it-s-really-like-67963eaa1119#.mlpmvg432.

force and the business take off? You'd have both missed out on a great opportunity to work together.

In other words, you have to tread lightly here. But that doesn't mean you need to give employees a rosy picture if everything isn't rosy, and remember—if things are really bad, they'll feel it anyway, and their anxiety will be exacerbated by not getting any information from you. I talk much more about this in chapter 9, on humility. What's more, there are situations in which your employees could be a great source of help and strength when you're struggling with a work-related issue. By opening up on appropriate work issues, you can let employees in and help let them know they are important and critical to the growth of the company. It helps them feel a sense of purpose. It gives them feelings of ownership in the company and a sense of control over their destiny. It also helps them feel comfortable opening up to you, because it reminds them that you are human. No one wants to deal with a robot who claims all is perfect when the wheels are coming off the bus.

If something's going wrong on the home front, or with your health, and you can't hide it at work, you can give your employees enough detail to know that neither they nor the company is the problem. Simply tell them that it's personal; that you don't feel like yourself. But the greater goal, of course, is to get the support you need so that when you go in to the office, you *can* be on. Or take the opportunity to go on leave for a bit.

Advisers and Mentors

Many entrepreneurs ask me if they should form an advisory group for their startups. I believe that a few great advisers, especially ones who have either run a startup or have a particular expertise that you don't have, can be incredibly helpful. However, be careful. Make sure you don't take on so many that you can't stay connected. Value quality over quantity. The best advisers are those who can make you and your company better, and that requires investment in the relationship and time spent together.

I'd also recommend shying away from a group advisory relationship, especially in the beginning of your company. Though it's beneficial to be part of a robust conversation with multiple opinions in the room, you're going to be exceptionally busy, and managing an advisory group takes a lot of time and coordination. You could always call a group meeting if a strategic issue comes up about which you could benefit from a debate. Then, when your company gets bigger, you can certainly bring on an advisory board or board of directors.

I also strongly recommend finding a coach, someone who will talk to you in complete confidence and advise you about maneuvering through all the rough patches you'll inevitably face. She can be an adviser, a mentor, or even a paid coach. Just make sure it's someone who will be able to speak both to the business struggles and personal struggles you're facing, because as I've said before and will say again, in the life of an entrepreneur, it's all intertwined. Make sure that your coach passes the Great Tribeship Test and that you feel you can be vulnerable with her or him.

Finding the ideal adviser isn't a simple matter. Part of it is old-fashioned networking. As an entrepreneur, you constantly have to be building your relationships. I have a friend, Rob, who would have coffee with one new person a week whom he didn't know. He didn't go into these meetings with any sort of agenda or purpose—he just wanted to get to know people and see what he might learn from them. He was genuinely curious about people, and he loved to learn. But part of what he was doing was cultivating the field of people he needed around him.

Depending on your relationship with your adviser, you both may be able to leverage a reciprocal relationship. I have a close friend, Susan, a high-energy, intelligent, experienced leader I worked for at Quaker Oats in 1996. She taught me how to manage a P&L and run a business, and she encouraged me to ask questions and learn. I always had great respect for her. We lost touch for a number of years, but we both ended up in San Francisco and reconnected when I was CEO of Clif and she was a marketing executive at Del Monte Foods. With a few former colleagues, she started a series of regular meetings for women she called the "Can Do" group, for the purpose of supporting each other in business, in life, and in friendship. Over time, we got really close. She wanted to be CEO for a long time, and I made sure I was her advocate however she needed me. I would send her frequent emails asking "How are you? What's the progress?" just to take her temperature. I wanted to be sure she was staying above the stressors. If I feared she was sinking down, I'd write and say, "Hey, let's get on the phone. Let's talk." She did the same for me, checking in frequently when I was going through my times with Blue Sky and Plum. Now that we're both CEOs of startups, we check in with one another every couple of weeks for five minutes. We talk about fundraising stresses, staff challenges, and more, and offer one another a shoulder to cry on. The key is, we both need that connection, and so it works. There are many ways to create reciprocity in a relationship.

In some scenarios, you might offer the person equity in the company. The key is to be very explicit about how often you want to talk to the other person, how accessible you want him or her to be, what sort of advice you're looking for, and how the relationship will be reciprocal.

I also believe strongly that you want advice to be uncomfortable sometimes. If your adviser is just a cheerleader who is going to think that everything you do is great, you're missing out. You want someone who is willing to push you, to probe and challenge you. I checked in with my friend and writing adviser Christine during my work on this book, and she pushed me hard in one telephone call on some really uncomfortable questions. There were several times during that call when I just wanted to hang up and run away from it, including her query about whether or not I was ready to face questions from readers about my anorexia. But she made me feel so safe, so unjudged. So I took a deep breath and jumped in fully by using her as a sounding board for other ideas that felt scary. It was a cathartic conversation that helped me to be sure that I was ready for several challenges to come in my life. Every good adviser should push this way. If they don't, you're not going to be able to effectively break through your blocks—and everyone has them.

Paid coaches and business therapists are becoming more and more popular in places like Silicon Valley, although we seem to still be caught in an old paradigm of separating business advice from therapeutic and wellness advice. When I mention the business therapist concept to other entrepreneurs, the typical response is "Hell yeah, sign me up!" I would even suggest that if you're a board member or investor, you can and should provide your leadership with such a coach.

At the very least, make sure they have a list of four or five people they can go to for confidential support. Set them up for success—because why wouldn't you? Even if they don't realize it in the beginning, the journey proves weary for even the toughest souls.

CHAPTER 4

Love in a Time of Churn

The Entrepreneur and Romance

S ara, a smart, thoughtful, and passionate student, came to see me during office hours when I was at Stanford GSB. I always loved office-hour time because the students would come in with their big dreams as well as their concerns. It was such a great way to get to know them on a personal level. Sara had a brilliant concept for a company, but she was struggling with how starting it would affect her relationship with her serious boyfriend, Paul. Paul wanted to move back home to New York. Sara wasn't sure if she should make the move to New York with him, when all her contacts for advice and potential funding were in San Francisco. Plus, was the relationship ready for this? And could she be both an entrepreneur and a loving girlfriend?

I said she was wise to consider the dedication it takes to launch a company. When someone is an entrepreneur, that person does not just have a "job." That "job" is in fact part of your family, and as a result, everyone needs to have a complete buy-in. "Is Paul willing to support you in how consuming it will be?" I asked.

She bit her lip. "I'm not sure. I'm not sure if he really gets it. You know, how hard it will be. On the other hand, am I too hung up on whether or not the relationship can work?"

"Are you willing to have the conversation with him about what the business will require of you and how important doing this startup is to you?" I pressed. The risk, of course, was that he might not be supportive.

Sara agreed to talk to Paul. But he wasn't the only one who had to commit to making it work. I asked if she was willing to create parameters herself around her work, in order to make space for the relationship. It would mean finding investors who were supportive of that space, and it would be challenging. It might mean saying no to certain investors. "That's tough," she said. "I'm not sure I could be that revealing about my personal life to a potential investor. Let me think about it." Several months later, Sara came to see me again and told me that Paul had been so encouraging that she was seriously considering moving with him and starting the company from New York. More important, it had opened up a vital dialogue in their relationship about their values and hopes for the future.

Sheila, another woman I advised, made a different choice. She wanted to engage in leading a growing company but didn't want to be consumed by it. She was looking at an opportunity to lead a company that was below $5 million in revenue (the range where you are really in startup mode and will need blasters to get the rocket off the launch pad with little fuel. After about $5 million, you have a little more fuel to use, and there are more investors interested in that size). I told her honestly that for at least a few years, the demands would be high in order to spur the company to a scalable model. She needed to be prepared and ready for the push, and she needed support from her board, her husband, Carl, and herself. Basically, I challenged her in a similar way to how I challenged Sara. In the end, she weighed these elements and decided to pass on the opportunity . . . this time.

Sheila wasn't wrong; Sara wasn't wrong—it's not a right-or-wrong situation. Rather, it's a matter of taking stock of your life and your values, and of being honest about what you need to be fulfilled as well as what your partner needs.

What I've set out to do in this chapter is to help you examine what it takes to have a romantic relationship and be an entrepreneur at the same time. It's not easy, and no one will tell you it is. Though statistics aren't kept about entrepreneurs' divorce rates, ask anyone in the field and they will describe the wreckage all around them. It's common sense, really: entrepreneurs often experience great financial strain, long hours, high stress, and extensive travel. It's hard to imagine a vocation that puts more strain on romantic life.

Much of what it takes to have a successful relationship when you are an entrepreneur is the same stuff it takes for any couple: commitment, love, understanding, respect. And yes, there are refrains of that advice in this chapter. But more important, there are traps that entrepreneurs are particularly susceptible to falling into, traps that, while they might not be wholly specific to entrepreneurship, have a very clear correlation with the profession.

If you're reading this and you're single, resist the urge to skip this chapter. You might think it doesn't apply to you, because you're single by choice while you focus on your endeavor.

But I don't believe that entrepreneurship and having a romantic relationship need to be mutually exclusive. You *can* have another central relationship in your life, other than that with your work. And chances are good that you will eventually have someone special in your life, even if you don't at the moment.

Trap 1: Not Sharing Buy-In

When I gave Sara the advice to talk to Paul about what her business would require of her, I was telling her to invite his buy-in. If you are bringing a startup into a serious relationship or marriage, it will affect everyone. As such, it cannot be strictly yours, or strictly your partner's. Entrepreneurs tend to forget this, because they're rewarded for wearing blinders—they see the target, and they forget that that's not all there is. Sometimes they use their startup as an excuse to be selfish, and that is unacceptable in a relationship. The startup must be a family goal, a shared goal. That doesn't mean both of you will be working on it each day, or that you'll both know about the nitty-gritty details, but you must both be invested.

I love the way my friend and REBBL investor Mark Rampolla, cofounder of Zico Coconut Water, and his wife, Maura, dealt with buy-in. Even though Mark and Maura had intertwined their finances in every other respect, he made sure she had shares of Zico in her name. It was a symbolic move that he said was one of the smartest things he did. "Right out of the gate, she clearly felt a sense of ownership," he said. And she needed to, in order to get them through the thin periods. "We had some really tough times the first couple of years; the business was struggling. One of those times was bad enough that we weren't sure we would be able to pay our mortgage.

We were one missed order or missed invoice away from losing our house. I remember sitting down with Maura and having a real conversation about that and saying, 'Look, I could get a job. We could figure this out.' She said, 'What would happen to my shares?'" She cared as much about Zico as Mark did, and having shares in her name was an important representation of that. In actuality, it really didn't matter whose name the shares were in, as they both owned all of them, but Mark had a brilliant way of making ownership feel real for Maura.

Kristin Richmond of Revolution Foods likewise said she and her husband, Steve, have that same shared buy-in. "We have been very clear with each other from day one that we wanted to have careers that we were passionate about and that we could reflect on and be proud of, and not just for financial reasons," she said. Steve is an entrepreneur, too, and has started three companies. But he is also a very real stakeholder in Revolution Foods. Since Kristin's job as CEO of a growing national company means that she has to travel several nights a month, it's important for their family that Steve has a job that keeps him local as much as possible. There have been times, Kristin said, where she's posited the hypothetical of the perfect job coming up for him that would require him to travel out of the country. But his interest is just as much in Revolution Foods as hers is; he maintained that he wanted to support them through Revolution Foods and would pursue his job search accordingly. "The cost of me stepping back [from Revolution Foods] right now is not a smart aligned goal, and Steve recognizes that as much as I do," she said.

For my part, I couldn't have gunned it as much as I did on Clif or Plum without Patrick handling so many of the details of our life. Patrick was really there every step of the way, just as I was there with him as he built Blue Sky. The goals weren't mine or his, they were ours, and if he hadn't been on board with my endeavors, I wouldn't have been able to pursue them. We are particularly fortunate in that we both come from not only the business world but the business-of-food world. Though it can backfire if all a couple does is talk about work, in our case it's been wonderful to have my best friend and partner also know exactly what I'm talking about when I mention ROI, or retailer charge backs, or using influencers to drive social media traffic. I'm also an adviser to a startup whose founder recently asked for my advice about brand positioning. Patrick happens to have expertise in that particular area and offered to talk to the founder. Patrick didn't do this for *me*—he did it for *us*, for our shared commitment that was our investment in this company.

While Patrick contributes his business brain like that all the time, he also contributes significantly on the domestic front. If one person does the heavy lifting at home while the other cranks hard on the startup, each is playing a critical role for both of them, and each should be valued for the contribution to the startup and to their lives. It's more complicated than simply saying, "Hey, I love you and value you, babe!" at the outset of the arrangement. It's a constant dialogue, a constant, "Can you pick up my dry cleaning today and thank you so much and I can stop at the store—do we need milk?" It's a constant patter of, "I know you're working really hard, and I am really in awe of your ability to do that."

Sometimes that shared investment is less about a monetary or business goal and more about what the family emotionally needs to thrive. There's a well-known Garth Brooks song, "Rodeo," about a woman who loves her cowboy, but he's in love with the rodeo. It brings him a fair share of pain, dust, and mud, but he *needs* it to be happy. I would posit that being an entrepreneur is a much more workable profession (we don't often break bones in our pursuits), but what ties the two together is that they are borne of passion, and they can mean a hard lifestyle.

Yardbarker's Pete Vlastelica is now an executive at Fox Sports, but he's not unlike the rodeo cowboy. "The desire to start another business is always there," his wife, Hilary, said of him. "Sometimes it's buried a little, but more often it comes up for air. Generating new ideas and seeking success is so built into Pete's DNA that for me to not support him would be me denying him something core to who he is. It's not just me being a supportive wife, it's me being happy when he's happy."

The anti-Hilary, of course, is the spouse who, instead of acknowledging and honoring that passion, resents it. Meg Cadoux Hirshberg, the wife of the legendary Stonyfield Farm founder Gary Hirshberg, wrote a column for *Inc.* about the toll entrepreneurship takes on families. One of her columns featured a CEO of a thriving PR agency whose husband became abusive as she became independent. "Of course, successful women in any profession risk similar backlash," Hirshberg wrote. "But entrepreneurs—by definition leaders of others— may pose a particular threat to vulnerable male egos."[*] While I would hope that situations in which abuse comes into play are rare, a relationship marked by competition seems much more common. Entrepreneurs like to win—that's the rush.

I'm lucky that ego and competition have never come into

[*]Meg Cadoux Hirshberg, "Why So Many Entrepreneurs Get Divorced," *Inc.*, November 1, 2010.

play with Patrick and me. Patrick is deeply grounded and satisfied as his own person. His concerns about my work are always rooted in his concerns about my well-being. When I went back to work at REBBL, we had long and serious conversations about what it would mean. He was skeptical for a while that it was the right thing for me or our family. He worried that it would harm my health, that it would bring too much stress, and that after a long week of work, I would be too tired to do anything all weekend. His buy-in took some time. In fact, at first I'd get jabs at dinnertime if I expressed that I'd had a hard day. We could have each retreated to our corners, hurt. But we talked about it. I said, "Patrick, I think what you're not understanding is that I am actually and truly enjoying this. Even though you see me working hard, at the end of the day, I'm happy. This is something that I really, really want to do, and if it gets to the point where it's not working, then we'll talk. But I need to do this."

"I just want you to be open to seeing if it's hurting you and us as a family," Patrick said. "I want you to be real about it." I told him that I understood, and that it was absolutely fair. With that honest conversation, we were both able to buy in. He had been looking at my working at REBBL through the lens of everything that was going to go wrong. Our conversation allowed him to see it differently; he now views REBBL as a great opportunity for me and for our family. He is ready to address it if something goes wrong, but he's not waiting for the other shoe to fall. And I know that I need to be diligent about my health and the impact of my work on our family. I need to be truly listening if Patrick says he's concerned. This was put to the test recently when I was feeling exhausted after a really rough couple of days. I was a little concerned about sharing my angst with Patrick because I was afraid he'd say, "Aha! I told you so!" But he was incredibly supportive. I shared my experience as well as my fear. He said, "Look, we all have bad days. I see how happy you are overall, and so I want to be there for you when it gets hard. I know that you'll be able to rest, reset, and jump back in. We'll both know if it's not working anymore."

The fact is, I love running companies. It's very consuming sometimes, but it gives me such an incredible high and is an important outlet for my intense energy. For example, when I decided to "retire early" when we moved to Santa Rosa, I had told my Stanford colleagues that I was just going to fingerpaint and read books for a while. Maybe find a philosophy discussion group to join. That lasted a couple of weeks. Then I joined the PTA board; shadowed a middle school counselor with the thought that perhaps I'd go back to school and start a second career; started teaching at Sonoma State; and joined various company and nonprofit boards. It's the way I'm wired.

That doesn't mean it's completely healthy—I still need to learn how to be still and alone with my thoughts, and that being on all the time doesn't mean I'm getting more done or that I'm a better person. I need to do as an entrepreneur friend of mine does, and when I feel that urge to accomplish as much as I can, to instead tell myself that "doing nothing is something." It's important—and healthy—to just be, and in a company, it allows you to be more thoughtful and to lead with a steady head and hand. I'll be the first to admit that I'm not great at it yet. If I'm not busy, I know I will have the space to reflect more inwardly and face some unexamined demons.

After twenty-five years together and almost twenty years of marriage, Patrick knows that my energy needs an outlet. And, though I may not be a fully actualized human being just yet, he agrees that I'm healthier and able to bring a more seasoned perspective to the craziness surrounding a startup. It makes him happy to see me happy right now. And, in due time, it will be time to let go completely and move into a different phase of life.

Imagine what would happen if both partners didn't feel a sense of ownership of the company, if you didn't have aligned goals. It's pretty easy to see: resentment of the financial inse- curity, resentment of the lack of time together, resentment of the attention one person is getting, resentment of how much is falling onto the other one's plate—or resentment that your dreams are stuck. When you each have buy-in, though, you're shooting for the same target, and supporting one another to get there.

Trap 2: The Blame Game

Blame is toxic in any marriage, and it's particularly threat- ening in the entrepreneurial sphere, where gambling is part of the deal and personal financial loss is a very real threat. I know more than a little about this topic. After Blue Sky fell apart and our family's finances were on the brink, people con- stantly asked me how Patrick and I managed to weather the storm together. And the answer is that we never blamed each other. For me, it would have been easy to take all my frustra- tion and fear out on him, as the person who started and over- saw the failed business. He has always been the first person to admit he made some pretty huge mistakes. Blaming him added no value. Patrick was hurting, and he was already so hard on himself. Piling on in order to alleviate my own stress would not have reflected the kindness and respect he and I have always held central to our marriage. I know how badly he wanted Blue Sky to work, and I encouraged him to go forward. How could we ever have trust in the future if I went back on my word? I love him deeply, and I've made plenty of misjudgments in my own life.

That doesn't mean I wasn't angry. But at the forefront of my mind was my concern with Patrick's well-being, which was deeply shaken. He frequently said to me, "You're going to get really mad one day," and though I denied it, he was right. Once Patrick was back on his feet, it hit me like a boulder. I think I had room to breathe and realize the full extent of our loss. I cried a lot. I was also depressed, since all the money I made at Clif had gone up in a puff of smoke. I lay on the floor and wailed. I couldn't believe it. Financial security had always been so critical to me, and I had worked hard to achieve it. Now it was all gone. I was out-of-my-mind angry.

For his part, Patrick accepted my unleashing of anger graciously. He was strongly committed to working through this setback in a healthy way. In his mind, he felt, *Phew, she's finally getting this out.* And I did. I expressed my anger, and then moved on. When I expressed my anger, it was like deflating a balloon that had been building inside me. It didn't take away my empathy for my husband. Blame is different— blame is a finger pointed in derision. Blame is a score settler, a conversation ender. With blame, couples stop talking to each other and instead get into a cycle of pride, denial, and self-protection.

Plus, I had an important role to play in Blue Sky's demise, too. I had (and have) so much respect and love for Patrick that when he asked me to support him and believe in his idea for

Blue Sky, I wanted to so badly that I did, blindly. In doing so, I ignored the warning signs that, as a businessperson, I might have been able to see otherwise, and that he probably would have been able to see if he hadn't been so deeply in love with the idea. I didn't want to be just another naysayer. When you get feedback on your startup, you become so used to being shot down. "That's an interesting idea," critics will say, "but with so many holes in it that you'll never make it float." Or "Well, maybe in a different era that would have worked, but never now." It's so easy to tear someone's idea down. But this was my husband, the father of my children, the love of my life—I wanted my role to be to build him up. I gave my complete blessing.

Our situation—two entrepreneurs, a disastrously failed business—might seem unique, but what underlies it is not. Storms like ours happen all the time. When they do, so many couples go through the blame game, and it works in both directions. If you are the partner who's not as closely associated with the startup, you might feel your entrepreneur is working too many hours, or taking too many risks, and the resentment builds up and up and up. You might be lonely, or worried about the financial future, or fed up with constantly canceled plans. You might feel abandoned, that you're not a priority— maybe even that you're taken for granted. You have a choice to make. You can ask your entrepreneur for what you need to be happy, or you can let your unhappiness turn into finger- pointing with a very clear target: the entrepreneur.

If you are the entrepreneur, you also have a choice. You might be stressed and lonely, too. There's a lot of pressure you're trying to absorb so that your employees, and your part- ner, don't have to feel it so acutely. You can hear your partner's

distress by stepping out of your own churn and listening. Take
that distress seriously and use it to start a discussion about
what each of you needs, where you can set limits on the business, and where you can't. Or you can interpret your partner's
bid for attention and love as just one more stressor that you
need to block out.

There's a healthy choice here, and a destructive one, and
no matter which side of the entrepreneurial romance you sit
on, it takes effort to make the healthy choice. I've been on
both sides myself. Patrick and I both know what it means to
work endless hours on a startup with no room to breathe, let
alone find time for somebody else. We both know what it's
like to be physically sitting with the one you love yet being
mentally in another universe. We both know how you can feel
that your startup is a complete reflection of you, and how that
slippery slope to obsession begins. And we know what it's like
to be on the other side of the table, missing the person you
love. So here's what I have to say to both sides:

Entrepreneurs—how can you not have empathy for your
partner? Do you know how freakin' hard it is, to hold down
the fort day after day? To perhaps be the breadwinner with
the stable job and feel like he has to keep it no matter how
miserable he may be in that job because you, as the entrepreneur, aren't going to be making up the difference in any short-
term time frame? Or to be the one who has to be on call on
the home front, since your own schedule is so unpredictable?
To manage financial fears or fears of the future? To watch
you go through the ups and downs of running a business? To
miss you and feel lonely when you're working? To feel like it's
all about you all the time? Tell your partner you love him, for
Pete's sake. Then show him you love him by being there for

him, as well. Make the time to communicate with him, and not just about the business and the to-do lists. Make sure he's happy. Tell him you understand how hard it is for him, and suggest he go to a support group for spouses of entrepreneurs. (Yes, they have them, such as through the Young Presidents' Organization and the Entrepreneurs' Organization.) It's true you have a lot on your plate, but it's not all about you.

Make it a priority to take the time to help your partner understand what you're going through. Make it vivid for him, so he can get it and better support you. Don't just assume that he won't understand. He can be your greatest source of support if you make your business part of your family and your family a supportive part of your business. And as important as the business is, also make sure you shut it down sometimes and listen to his needs.

Partners—how can you not have empathy for your entrepreneur? She feels the weight of the world on her shoulders some days. She wants to please her business partners, investors, employees, and customers. She has to make an endless stream of decisions and isn't at all sure they're the right ones sometimes. She worries about failing you and feels guilty she's not more available. She worries she's putting your lives in a holding pattern, or that something will happen and it will all fall apart. Tell her you love her. Better yet, make sure you show her you love her by listening with empathy and helping her get through the rough patches.

Really talk to each other and stay connected, even if for short spurts of time. You can't put a marriage or a significant relationship on hold, no matter how much you'll likely want to do so at times. Remember, you are going through this experience together whether you want to face that fact or not. And if you don't face it, you risk being another divorce statistic. Yes, it's stressful, as you can see from both sides. Yes, maybe there is financial loss and loneliness, but blame has no place and "*fault*" is an f-word in every sense. Don't use it.

Trap 3: Making Time

As with many entrepreneurs, my days are a blur of meetings and piles of tasks, and my time is scheduled to the minute. Yet I'm committed to doing everything I need to within a nine-hour workday, and anything that can't get done in that time has to wait. It's kind of crazy that entrepreneurs think we have to work as much as we do. Yes, there's a ton that needs to get done, but if you're really practical about it, it's easy to see that you're simply not effective after working for hours on end. But especially when there's investor money on the line, you think you need to spend every waking minute focused on the business. That's just wrongheaded. Let go of guilt and, like any good businessperson, focus on *effectiveness*. When do you stop being effective? Perhaps you tell your partner you have to skip your dinner date because you have too much to do, but really think about it: in the hour it would take you to have dinner, you could recharge, strengthen your relationship, eat some healthy food, and refresh your brain. Spend that hour at work and you'll feel like you've really gunned it for the company, but when you've been at it for sixteen hours straight, your effectiveness, your health, your relationship, and your ability to approach your work creatively will take a hit. So what's the better choice for the net positive?

"I had a pretty steep diminishing margin of returns on my efforts," Mark said of his time at Zico. "After eleven or twelve hours, I'm worthless. And any decisions I make are probably not going to be the best ones." So he got to the point where he was home for dinner every night. He was adamant about keeping Sunday clear, and he took a vacation each year. Giving his wife and family the priority they deserved, he said, forced him to get really clear on the priorities of the business, too. "I'd ask, 'What are the four things I want to accomplish this year? If I want to get those four things done, what do I need to get done this month? This week? This day? I was very disciplined about prioritization."

Otis and Elizabeth Chandler, a married couple, are the cofounders of Goodreads, and as the business has grown and their family has grown (they have an infant, a two-year-old, and a five-year-old), Elizabeth said, "We've had to become more deliberate about how we work." They were influenced by the book *The Power of Habit*, and one of the habits they've developed is putting their phones down as soon as they get home from work. More work might be done after the kids go to sleep, but from dinnertime until then, it's family time. They also have a regular Thursday date night, which they make a priority in their schedule, and committing to this has meant that they have always stayed closely connected as a couple through the challenges of starting and growing a business.

Like these other couples, Patrick and I are always adamant about having dinner together as a family every night. Then he and I stay at the table for twenty minutes after we excuse the kids, just so we can talk alone and catch up. Every Friday and Saturday late afternoon, we have happy hour together. We sit, have a glass of wine, and talk. Even when the kids were young and we were working a lot, we took trips alone together. We believed strongly in how we prioritized our relationship. We also had parents who were role models, who had beautiful, long-lasting romances with one another. Patrick's father still refers to his wife as "my bride," and they've been married almost sixty years. My mom and dad adore each other and have always been committed to going out to dinner every Wednesday and Saturday night since the day they met. We understood that our parents' relationship was fundamental to our families' well-being, and our boys understand that about us, too.

I've learned a lot, too, about how slowing down and being with my family has been helpful for REBBL and has encouraged me to work smarter. I used to go on overdrive and answer emails immediately in order to clear them off my plate. Sometimes that worked, but other times it was ineffective, since I wasn't fully reading and digesting what was being asked of me. Then I'd send the rest of my team running around in circles. I've learned to slow down the pace enough to be thoughtful and, when I can't process fully any longer, I shut it down. As I've practiced this, it hasn't made me any busier. In fact, it's made me less busy, because an issue is more likely to be sufficiently resolved than to become a round-and-round email circle.

Patrick and I still talk about how to give work the right amount of focus while giving our relationship and our family the nurturing time it needs. Patrick would like it if I didn't use up quite so much of my energy during the week so that I'm too zonked to go out on Fridays. But we do often go out on dates on Saturday nights, have guests over, or find an excuse to have a family party. This weekend we are celebrating a belated Saint Patrick's Day and both kids' great report cards. There are always good reasons to celebrate the family. Most important, I put limits on the time I work during the week, so I have energy for my family that I didn't used to have, and I am clear about minimizing the work I have to do on weekends, avoiding it completely if I can. I preserve family time, which helps my employees, too—if I work on the weekends, it sets a standard that they have to do so, too—and I don't want that for any of us. Recently at REBBL, we implemented a no-Friday-meeting rule and a no-email-on-the-weekend rule. If there's an emergency, a text is sent out, but it's got to be a true emergency. (Tip: These ground rules are important because, without them, people follow your lead whether you want them to or not. Just saying "I don't expect you to work as much as me" is not enough. Your behaviors mean more than your words.)

Patrick and I have been through a lot together, and at the risk of sounding terribly cheesy, I have to say that I love him more every day and every year we spend together. I'm inordinately proud of us and the way we've grown stronger through all the bumps of life. There's a lot that's gone into it, of course, but our happy hour ritual is a critical part of how we've managed that growth; it signifies our prioritization of our relationship through thick and thin. When I was at Clif, Patrick and I had our happy hour wine in our living room, holding hands on the couch in front of the fireplace. When Blue Sky fell apart, we moved to a town house in Fremont on a patch of land right off of I-680, with less than eight feet of space between houses. To make do, since we had no yard, we pulled folding chairs out to the driveway and had our happy hour to the sounds of freeway traffic. We didn't know for sure that we'd ever dig out of our financial hole, but we did. And now we have our happy hour on our back patio in wine country overlooking the hills, watching the most awe-inspiring sunsets I've ever seen. We are still in conversation with each other, and it turns out we still have a lot to say.

Trap 4: Losing Track of Values

Underlying each and every one of the points I've made in this chapter is the need to share values. From values come shared goals and buy-in. From values comes empathy instead of blame. From values come prioritizing family and relationships over business. If you haven't had a serious talk with your partner about values, or if you haven't refreshed the conversation in a while, it's important to sit down and talk, regardless of the chaos around you. This conversation is the foundation of your future.

Pete and Hilary were in their midtwenties and childless when Pete started Yardbarker. They had always loved traveling together, as they both had a bit of wanderlust. Then when Pete was in the throes of growing the company, a close friend invited them to his wedding in Scotland. "I remember thinking the wedding was unfortunate, that it was as far away as it was," said Pete. It would mean taking time off work, which was a huge ask during that period. Though they had to take three planes to get there, they stayed in Scotland for only two days. Hilary wanted to stop over in London on the way home to visit family. Pete resisted, but Hilary talked him into it.

"When we were on our way to London, he turned into this angry person," Hilary said. "We were only there for a day and a half, but Pete said, 'I told you I had to get back for work and you made me go through London.' To me, we'd taken this long trip and took a one-day stopover. It just made sense to do. But to him, he was so entrenched that it was a really stressful day for him. It was interesting, and upsetting. I remember saying, 'Do I ever get you back? Is this going to be it forever?'"

Mark Rampolla and his wife sat down before he started Zico Coconut Water to talk about what it would mean for their life together, and how they would recognize they were on the right path. "If someone wants to build a [financially] successful business and that's what it's all about, there's nothing wrong with that," said Mark. "But I think most entrepreneurs don't really think through what the consequences are. From the beginning, [my wife and I] were clear on what was a loss, no matter how much money or notoriety came from the business: if I die of a heart attack at fifty-five, if we get a divorce, if our children are miserable and not well raised and don't have perspective on life, that's a loss. If I'm healthy, we have a great marriage, our kids are thriving—that became the bottom end of success." Writing it down was key for them, and Mark said he even kept score, noting how many nights he was home for dinner. Even with all that intent and forethought, he said, he still frequently needed his wife to kick him in the pants. "It took my wife reminding me of this again and again, asking, 'Hey, what is this really all about?'" he said. "It's really easy for entrepreneurs to lose track of that." Importantly, it was relatively easy for his wife to do this because she wasn't nagging—she was simply reminding him of the values they'd agreed upon, and that they'd agreed they'd each uphold.

In my relationship, Patrick is the one who most often needs to remind me of our agreement. Similar to Mark and his wife, Patrick and I did an exercise together in which we wrote down our family values, and then sat down with the kids and talked about each value, what it means to us, and how the kids feel about it. The biggest priority for us is loving—loving each other and ourselves. We agreed that to have time for loving each other, we can't be all about work all the time. We need to make room for each other. Dinner together is not an option, it's a given. After dinner, I attack a few more work things. But when it's gone on too long, especially past eight thirty, Patrick says "shut it down" so that we can spend some time together. I cringe, both because I don't really want to shut it down (I just want to check that one—no, two—last emails) and because I know he's right. He's keeping me true to our values, because loving myself means taking care of myself—which means getting enough rest. That's why "that's enough," are two of the most powerful words either of us can say to the other.

Patrick is also especially conscious of signs of the old behaviors that led to my anorexia. He can see when I'm in overdrive. The sure signs are when I'm starting to move too fast, when I'm not being thoughtful about what I'm eating, or when I'm working out too much. He pulls me back, which is helping me to better acknowledge these tendencies in myself and stop them. It's so easy to ignore this stuff as an entrepreneur, since it's just more to deal with. Who has time to be conscientious? However, I know that my health, my family, and my company depend on my taking the time to address it. It's a value that Patrick holds me to. He's my higher consciousness, and my job is to make sure that he doesn't have to do that all the time, so we can both be at peace with our lives.

One of the most poignant questions you can ask yourself, and your partner, is what Mark's wife asked him regularly: "Hey, what is this really all about?" In the answer to that question lies awareness, thoughtfulness, and perspective. There is an urge to keep moving everything forward all the time, but when you don't stop to ask that question, you might well be exhausting yourself for all the wrong reasons. Asking that question keeps you grounded and reminds you of the mission statement you have for your *life*.

Recently my son Connor was working on one of those geologic time lines for school that show the important events in earth's history relative to how long they lasted. Human life on earth is miniscule compared with the time before there was any life on the planet, or when there were dinosaurs. Each of us is such a wisp of that time. Patrick and I talk about how we need to best use that wisp, and to me, it's not about the hours I spent on that board meeting and how I perfected that speech.

Since an entrepreneurial endeavor is a family endeavor, don't shortcut the tough conversations about what it will mean. Mark Rampolla said he and his wife, Maura, planned almost as much for how the startup would work into their family life as he spent planning for the startup itself. But this planning is key. Toward that end, here are some questions and discussion points to get you started:

- How long can you sustain the startup lifestyle?
- What does that mean for your significant other's life goals?
- What financial sacrifices are you each willing to make, and for how long?
- What will constitute success for the business, and what will be considered the time to walk away from sunk costs?
- What would be some indicators that your venture wasn't successful?
- How will you each cope with loneliness?
- What values that you treasure as a couple must you give up? For how long?

- What are you not willing to give up?
- What does success mean to the two of you? Do you agree with one another?
- What are the early years of a startup going to require of each of you? What limits can you set on work hours? What level of travel can you live with? How will you make time for each other, for your family? And, how do you make sure that your significant other can call you out on your shit without your getting defensive?

These are the key questions every couple should answer at the outset, so that they don't find themselves fighting over a stopover in London, confused about when they stopped valuing travel the same way. So they don't find themselves as ships passing in the night with no connection. So that resentments don't start to bubble up unaddressed, leading to the end of the relationship. Though it takes work, the time and energy put in reaps a return on investment that leads to a happy life.

CHAPTER 5

My Baby You'll Be

The Entrepreneur and Children

I n the movie *The Intern*, starring Anne Hathaway and Robert De Niro, Hathaway plays a young mother and the founder of a growing e-commerce business. When other moms at school remind her about a class potluck, they tell her she can buy the guacamole, since she's so busy. The implication is that they are snubbing her, and she takes it as such. She insists she can make the guacamole, though *when* is anyone's guess. Her husband stays home with their daughter, which Hathaway's character is unendingly grateful for, and even fights the feeling that she's to blame if he's dissatisfied or disconnected. It takes the perspective of a retired widower (Robert De Niro) to show her how unjust it all is. While yes, it's only a movie, it also struck me as a very accurate snapshot of the stressed-out, "I must be all things to all people" reality of momtrepreneurs.

It's heartening that Hollywood is willing to acknowledge that moms are entrepreneurs and that dads can do the work at home. It's these messages that reflect and shape a changing reality. Yet we need to find better solutions to take away the stigma that many moms feel at work, and that many dads feel while staying at home. We need a new paradigm.

In twenty years, when a book written by a woman entrepreneur comes out, it's my hope that it will look very different. For one, she won't even be identified as a "woman entrepreneur." She will just be, simply, an entrepreneur. In this future I see, boardrooms will be filled with equal numbers of men and women, and so will PTA meetings. In this future, when I take questions from a lecture hall of eager faces, a young man will stand up and say, "I'm worried about having a baby when I have to work so much. What if I have to miss a well-child check or something? What will I do if there's an event at preschool and an investor meeting at the same time?"

We're not yet at the point where the stresses of being a working parent is a gender-neutral issue, and we're an even longer way from it ceasing to be an issue at all. Working moms feel the stress acutely. A recent study from the Pew Research Center found that 41 percent of adults think the increase in working mothers is bad for society, while only 22 percent say it's good.[*] In other words, women feel pressure and judgment, and it's not only in their heads—people *are* making judgments, and sometimes not with much subtlety. This is the current landscape for working moms, like it or not. Imagine the terrain like that of a mountain bike path—bumpy, rocky, and with overgrown roots jumping out at any given moment, ready to throw you off balance and off your bike. Now imagine that your bike has only one wheel—and that's what it is to be a working mom who also happens to be an entrepreneur. Being a dad and an entrepreneur isn't easy, either, and plenty

[*] "Fewer Mothers Prefer Full-time Work," Pew Research Center, July 12, 2007.

of the themes in this chapter apply to fathers, too. We all feel pressures and stereotypes about gender roles; men miss out on family life because of those stereotypes, just as women are guilt ridden by them.

When I was CEO of Clif Bar, I was able to balance my family life and work life pretty well, thanks in large part to Patrick's covering more on the home front. I thought, *Huh. I guess I'm pretty good at this whole balance thing. Go, Sheryl!* When I cofounded Plum, I didn't think it would be that much more difficult. I was wrong. I hadn't realized how much *help* I'd had at Clif, just by virtue of having so many people, structures, and systems already established. (Need to get a new product done? Get the research and development team working on it. Need to sell a product? Contact the sales team. Need market research? Easy—send a request to the person who plays that role! Need a tech person? He's right down the hall. Want to mail something out right away? Your assistant takes care of it, then the mailroom packs, sends, and tracks it.) At Plum, it was only Neil, me, and our good friend Bentley Hall, and we were putting everything together from scratch, from buying the dishes for our work kitchen to installing the computers to hanging shelves on the walls while we cranked out spreadsheets, wrote presentations, called potential investors, and had in-depth interviews with moms. As we grew, we brought in just enough people to keep us afloat but not enough people to enable delegation, a typical startup scenario.

On the one hand, I had flexibility with my work hours at Plum. I could choose when to get to the office and when to leave. Once we had a team in place, I tried to be conscious of not setting an around-the-clock example. However, I was always, always working. Even when I was home with the kids, I was thinking about work—and as any working parent knows, that's the worst. It was all-consuming, and I never felt I could turn it off. I felt guilty when I was with my kids that I wasn't doing something for Plum (I knew that Neil probably was). I felt guilty for the hours I spent at work when I was missing something of my kids', when other moms I knew were always at every kid event. I won't go on, because this is the most common refrain in the book of working moms. You've heard it before, but it hurt, and it was hard.

Know—and Be—Who You Are

It's imperative and freeing to recognize that both women and men have choices. We can all spend time working outside and inside the house. Instead of wasting energy feeling guilty about our choices, we should focus our efforts on flourishing in any endeavor we choose and letting go of perfect, because perfect's just a mirage. But of course, this is all easier said than done, right? Let me tell you how I learned this the hard way.

After I had Connor, I was on leave for two months from Clif Bar. Wanting to meet other moms, I joined the Golden Gate Mother's Club, which is a huge gathering of San Francisco–area moms. Out of roughly a hundred moms at the first meeting, only eight of us were working moms, and we were grouped together. We're still in touch with one another sixteen years later. Jokingly, we called ourselves the "Mean Mommies," ironically not because we felt we were evil or something for working, but because we all could get a little ornery at times when we were maxed out, and we all had a tendency to call a spade a spade. All the other moms we knew were so sugary sweet and would express how blissful motherhood was all the time. We didn't identify with them at all.

When Connor was eight and Gavin five, another Mean Mommy and I carpooled to a gathering of our group. On the drive there, she turned to me and said "You know, Sheryl, we"—the "we" presumably being all the other moms in the group—"don't understand your lifestyle. You do the hardcore career thing and never spend time with your kids. You also focus on your spousal relationship at a detriment to your kids." The Mean Mommy gun was now pointed at me. I couldn't say a thing. I was shocked and started crying. These were the friends I had been hanging out with for years. I was embarrassed and horrified that I had to spend the night with these women, who apparently thought I was doing such a shit job. When I got to our friend's house to join the rest of the gang, I was still shaken up. I told them what this friend had said in the car, sure that they would deny it. Instead I was greeted with some uncomfortable shifting of feet and heads looking down at shoes. It was agonizing to hang out there that whole evening and to have to drive back home with the friend who had decided that "sharing was caring."

Somehow I made it through the evening, and the second I got home, I called Patrick, who was out of town. Patrick, with his calm self-assurance, said, "Sheryl, this is our life and our choice. We believe in our choice. It doesn't matter what they say."

I heard him that night and tried to internalize his confidence. Who cared what anyone else thought? And this friend was wrong—my kids were doing great, I was engaged with their lives, and my strong marriage to their father was a wonderful example for them, as well as a sturdy foundation for our whole family. I knew this to be true, but for a long time, I still felt guilty. So when we moved to Santa Rosa and I no longer had a full-time day job, I was thrilled to be able to throw myself into all the things I felt guilty for missing out on over the years. School drop-offs and pickups, folding laundry, making cookies, and setting playdates. You name it—I did it. I even joined the board of the PTA. And here's what I found: I hated it. I sat in PTA meetings, forcing myself to pay attention to the agenda, all the while knowing that it wasn't the place for me. The other board members were wonderful, smart, creative volunteers—I don't want to take anything away from their good work. It just wasn't *my* work. This, too, made me feel guilty, so I added that to the list. I loved my kids and wanted to be with them, but I didn't have the ease that Patrick always seemed to have in their world, or the interest that the other PTA parents had in everything that went on at the school. I wondered what was wrong with me.

It took a long time and plenty of soul-searching for me to really *get* what Patrick had said that night years before: "This is our life and our choice. We believe in our choice." This wasn't a realization that happened overnight or after one conversation. Rather, it came from talking to other moms who expressed challenges with managing it all and realizing I cut them a lot more slack than I cut myself. It came from connecting with people who were willing to say what was real, what was hard. And it came from paying attention to my kids, and how they were responding to us as parents and developing their own philosophies and values. For instance, on one wedding anniversary, our kids wrote Patrick and me a card that reflected what we'd been trying to teach them for years about love, compassion, and caring. Connor wrote, "Thank you for everything you two have gone through to stay together and raise us. . . . I will always look to you two as a guideline for love because of how you are together." And Gavin wrote, "Your caring has stopped a great fall. From the deepest depths of my heart, I thank you for never drifting apart."

Over time, I came to believe that there's not just one way to be a good mom. I had to accept that I needed to be myself, and own what it was I loved to do—which was to run a company. Then I had to figure out a way to share that with my kids in a way that would be a meaningful example to them. I've found some ways to do that. Connor's middle school culinary teacher invited me in to talk about food companies. As I walked in, Connor gave me the biggest hug and kiss in front of all the middle schoolers who were piling into the room. As I spoke, he sat right near the front of the class and grinned from ear to ear. I could feel my heart skip with such love.

I also share a lot about my work life with my kids, and so does Patrick. We share the joys and the hardships so they can celebrate with us and understand what is great and also what is challenging about adult life. Plus, it shows them who we are, as full human beings, and helps them understand what drives us and motivates us. Mihaly Csikszentmihalyi, the author of the bestselling book *Flow*, defines "flow" as "the state in which people are so involved in an activity that nothing else seems to matter; the experience itself is so enjoyable that people will do it even at great cost, for the sheer sake of doing it.""* (Importantly, he does not feel that you can be in a state of flow all the time, but he does believe that having those peak moments is key to finding fulfillment.) In the book, he talks about the importance of children seeing adults involved passionately with their work and life. He encourages parents to not be helicopter parents, whose lives become completely immersed in their children. The impression it can leave on kids is "Why should I want to become an adult? It's so boring!" It's critical for us to remember that when we are whole, our children learn how to become whole.

There's a bestselling children's book called *Love You Forever* that my sister-in-law bought for me when Connor was born. In its first pages, a young woman holds her newborn son and sings about how she'll love him forever and like him "for always":

"As long as I'm living

My baby you'll be."

To this day I can't read that book without crying, and my kids know it. That passage is like a guiding light to me. My kids know how desperately I love them, and at the end of the day, I think that's the best thing I can do as a mom. I don't make cookies much nowadays, and I'll never join the PTA again, but I find other ways to give that mean more to me. And I don't feel guilty anymore. Interestingly, the friend of mine who made me cry on the way to the Mean Mommies meetup? She later told me how wrong she was, that she actually saw that I was right to prioritize my relationship with Patrick. I'm good friends with her and the rest of the group

*Mihaly Csikszentmihalyi, *Flow: The Psychology of Optimal Experience* (New York: Harper and Row, 1990).

to this day, and in the end, the encounter and its resolution taught me something really valuable about having confidence in my choices.

That was my long way to finding where I fit as a mom and as an entrepreneur, and it felt very right once I owned it. All parents have to do this, whether they come to the decision that they want to work more, less, or not at all—and assuming that they are in the fortunate position to have a choice in the first place.

Julie Schlosser was a writer and then an editor at *Fortune* before leaving to start her own company. She and another former *Fortune* writer, Lee Clifford, cofounded Altruette, a jewelry company that supports nonprofits. They had their launch at the upscale clothing store Fred Segal, and were featured by *O* magazine and *InStyle* in their second year. Lee and Julie also started their families at the same time they started Altruette—both women now have two young children—and its growth has been slower because of it. "I could have a large company and one child or a large company and no child," Julie said. But she's completely happy with where she is, with a small company and two small boys. "Maybe it's because I waited until I was older to have kids," she said, "but this feels fulfilling at this stage in my life."

Julie is the first to admit that she is lucky to get the chance to raise her children. She realizes that not all women have the financial flexibility. The point remains, nonetheless: she is an ambitious businesswoman with a viable company, and she's intentionally taking the ride in a lower gear. In fact, she and Lee both want to keep their flexible, part-time schedules, and are looking to hire someone who will be able to commit full-time to Altruette. In time, Julie will ramp up. But she's confident in the choice she's made for now. "Altruette is really my third child," she said. "Sometimes she gets more attention than the boys. Sometimes it's the other way around. It's constant juggling, and you do feel that you are constantly short-changing one of them. That said, they each help me keep a balanced perspective on life. When things at home get crazy (sick kids, fussy kids, etc.), focusing on building Altruette is a bit of heaven. And when challenges arise at Altruette, an afternoon of building bridges with my boys creates a wonderful sense of calm and contentment."

I love that Julie has found her groove and that she owns it. The more we can create our lives around us and our family and resist the pressure of what others expect, the happier we'll be, and the better example we'll set for our kids. The main point is not to endorse Julie's route or my route or any other parent's route. Rather, it's that you should recognize that gendered pressure exists, and that the mommy wars, while they may have tamed, are real. Knowing that this judgment is swirling in the atmosphere, plant your feet firmly. Decide who you are, what you believe, and what works for you. And, as nicely as you can, tell everyone else to back the hell off.

Assess the Whole Ecosystem

Instead of thinking about startups versus parenthood as a scale with a weight on either end, look at it instead like an ecosystem, and one that fluctuates all the time. You can't just look at yourself; when you are part of a family, you no longer operate in a vacuum. And you can't just look at the present; life changes, and a family's needs change.

So start this way: look at the big picture of your life and

ask, "Can I be truly sustained seeing my kids this little of the time? Can they be? For how long?" Perhaps you have enough of a network in place that the kids are doing great, and though you're not able to be with them as much as you'd like, you're able to really focus on them when you are together. Your ecosystem's working. But often the answer is no—either your kids can't be sustained or you can't—and then you have a choice to make.

Toward the end of my time at Plum, my answer was no, that I could not be sustained being with my kids so little, physically and mentally. So I took stock. They were growing up without me, and, as they were becoming teenagers, I wanted to be more connected. I realized that while I could grow Plum for a time, I could not stay with the company to the next stage. I also saw that I didn't want to be a serial founder. In a way, it made the stakes with Plum feel even higher, because I understood that this was it—this would be my only business that I would give birth to. In so many ways, it had been a deeply rewarding chapter—but I needed to see more of my kids in the next chapter.

At a gathering of advisers for an innovative new food conference called the Harvest Summit, I met a bubbly fellow adviser, Lauren Belden, and we hit it off immediately. Lauren and her husband, Nate, had recently left thriving careers in branding and finance to start a wine label, Belden Barns. At the same time she was helping build the label, Lauren was also involved in several other entrepreneurial endeavors, all of which excited her. Put together, though, it was too much, and not only did it make her feel too separated from her kids, it sent Lauren into a serious bout of insomnia and anxiety.

Lauren was home alone with their two young kids one

night while Nate was out of town for the business. At one point, her son Milo—who wasn't yet two—was just inconsolable, and Lauren couldn't put her finger on why, nor could she soothe him. Lauren tried everything to calm him down—all the old tricks she'd once employed to perfection—and nothing worked. "It's scary not to be able to comfort your own child," she said. "I saw I needed to spend more time with this guy. It was a wake-up call for what I really wanted and needed emotionally at that point." Since that moment, she said, "I've really had to change my approach and make peace with the fact that maybe all your dreams can come true, but maybe not at the same time. You have to recognize your limits as a human being."

This "not at the same time" refrain is key. Entrepreneurs tend to feel they have to be everyone and do everything at once, but they need to recognize and fight that impulse. This type of thinking really helped Julie Schlosser. Altruette might be in low gear for now, but that doesn't mean it will be forever. She has a great role model for thinking this way. Her mom had a career as a schoolteacher before she had kids. She stayed home with Julie and her brother, but then she had a fantastic third act working at a university, where she grew her role and the scope of her job through the years.

No matter where you are with your venture or what you choose about your family life, there are a few hard questions that must be answered honestly:

1. How much time can you spend on your work and be healthy? Are you getting enough time with your family so that you feel grounded and that you're living in accordance with your values? It may sound like a leading line

of questioning, but I assure you it's not. Plenty of people would answer yes. They know themselves well, and they're right. But really ask yourself, and ask others who can hold a mirror up to you as well. When I wasn't spending enough time with my kids, I knew it. I was working a lot, and even when I was home, I was distracted. The boys became very, very close with Patrick, and it almost felt like they didn't know me. I could feel in my gut that there was a distance, and I was like an outsider. Anything that had to be done, they asked Patrick to do. They didn't ask me. I knew something was wrong—they just didn't expect me to be available. It wasn't a healthy place for me or them to be.

2. Can your family give you the space to go hard and remain healthy themselves? Again, in some families, the answer is yes—for a time. Even so, you can't block out your family completely. That's not fair to them, and you need the connection and support that only family, or friends who are like family, can provide. The voices of the past are filled with people who regretted not spending enough time with their kids. Let's learn from them. Are your kids showing signs that they are struggling with school, or with friends? Are you clearing your head enough to be able to be with them when they do? One of my closest friends from my Stanford days, Sharon, shared some sage advice with me when I asked her how to get my teenage son to talk to me. "Don't get him to talk, just be there when he's ready, even if it's three a.m." Of course, it's impossible to always be available, but if you *never* are, really ask yourself if those who need you are floating too far away.

3. Can you hold yourself to a time limit for going hard?

4. Can you involve your children in the business in ways that are inspiring to them, so they see you as a role model as opposed to an absent and distant parent?

Build a Team

Many people feel uncomfortable starting a business and a family near, or at, the same time. But like it or not, human reproduction has a season that's determined for us. So for those who go for it, I say that you can be a parent, an entrepreneur, and a sane person at the same time—but not unless you have a team.

Kristin Groos Richmond of Revolution Foods is a cofounder and CEO, and she has two young kids. She had her oldest child, now ten, on the day she signed the term sheet for Revolution Foods' first financing. She is an undisputed rock star in her field, and yet that doesn't make her impervious to pressure. When the intensity mounts, she's learned to ask how much she's putting on herself, and how much is *really* there. And, like all of us, she had to have a moment of complete and utter honesty with herself about where she was going to plant her feet. "Inside myself, I owned what I thought was reasonable in the balance of being a good mom and being a CEO of a rapid-growth, values-driven company. I knew that it's more than a full-time job, and I needed to find a way to make it work for myself, my family, my team, and my board." Her cofounder, Kirsten Tobey, started her family at the same time, and the two women supported each other, encouraging the other to take maternity leave and to take vacations with their families. Kirsten is a big part of Kristin's team, and vice versa.

Of critical importance on this team, of course, is your partner, if you have one. (And if you don't, then the important person is whoever is helping you with the kids.) Patrick has a thriving business career of his own, but at times when I was crunching on Plum, he was able and willing to be the primary parent, the one who cut meetings short to pick up the kids, or who missed a day of work if one of our boys was sick. We were very clear about what our roles would be, and we stuck to them. Sometimes the way he did things made me crazy. Entrepreneurs tend to be go-getters, and we also tend to like things to be done a certain way. I had to learn to let go—our family was not going to fall apart because a pan was dirty. It was Patrick's right to run things how he pleased, as long as they were done in accordance with our mutual values. That was our deal. And sometimes I know my hours made him equally nuts, and he had to learn to recognize when I was overdoing it and when I really did need to be working that much.

Second, you have to make sure your investors or your board are part of the team. If possible, let them know at the outset that you intend to set boundaries on your work life so that you can enjoy your family. Help them see that it will get them a better you, and if they don't see that or agree to that, then reconsider whether you want them to be part of your team. Once they've agreed to a standard, hold on to it. Excepting emergencies, don't take calls when you're putting your kids down for bed. If an investor or board member gives you a hard time about your inaccessibility after hours, remind them of the expectations you set out at the get-go. Hold the line and don't feel sorry for an instant. I learned this the hard way when I had an investor board member who would call me on the weekends. He was actually a family man, so he may have understood if I told him my parameters. But I didn't. Before I joined REBBL, I was very clear with my board that my family is very important to me and I must have parameters around my work. They've been very supportive, and it helps me each day to know that I don't need to tiptoe when I have family priorities I need to take care of.

Kristin also maintains clear boundaries and is unapologetic about things like avoiding client or investor dinners when she's not traveling. "I asked myself, what work meeting truly has to happen over dinner?" she said. She holds that time sacred for her family—she can meet investors or key clients for breakfast or lunch. And she's equally committed to taking all her vacation time. "I'm very forthcoming with my team and investors about how I am taking each day of my vacation, and I'll often say, 'I'm completely unplugged on this one.' I explain my desire to have presence with my family, and that's going to make me perform better." A great adviser or teammate understands this, and she recently had one of her largest investors tell her, "Kris, the goal is to have you working less hours, not more, so that you can be with those little boys more. Build your team up to make them as effective as possible to allow you to have a more balanced work life." Kristin acknowledges that the job is demanding and the intensity is always high in her role, but that these strategies help keep her "in the game" to build a lasting company with the impact she seeks.

Which brings me to the third category on your team: those you work with. Are they going to pick up the ball and run with it so you can go to the science fair? Are you *letting* them? And are you reciprocating? If you're working with someone who doesn't have a significant other or kids, it's still equally important for them to take time for personal priorities. Sometimes parents think they're the only ones who have priorities. Assure your team that you understand the importance of their lives, no matter who or what is in them.

It's important to challenge yourself as leader as your venture grows to ensure you're delegating instead of trying to do it all yourself, thinking that only you know the best way to do it, because—surprise!—that's not so. This is hard for many entrepreneurs, because what made you successful in the beginning was your sheer force of will and your ability to make it happen yourself. Letting go of pieces of the company demonstrates your capability as a leader, and it is deeply motivating to your people and very welcome to your family.

Be Present

When I was at Plum, Patrick and I determined the amount of time that was reasonable for me to be at work versus at home, and I tried to stick to it. I was home for dinner most of the time; I made sure I was there for Friday-night drinks, date night Saturdays, and Sundays for family all day. But even when I wasn't looking at my work emails, I *thought* about Plum constantly—when I was in the shower, when I was at my kids' sports games, when I was having a meal with them, or when I was chilling in front of the television with Patrick. I was always a million miles away, and I needed to find a way to turn it off.

Everybody has a different way to do this. Kristin will meditate on the Richmond Bridge, or listen to *Radiolab* on public radio—whatever she has to do to make the transition she needs in order to leave work at work. I'm not always great at compartmentalizing even to this day, but have found that if I can write down whatever it is that I'm stewing over at work, I can release it, and it helps me re-center. I hate running to my computer during weekend time, but sometimes it makes sense to—if I can knock out thirty minutes of work that will clear my head and allow me to be present for the rest of the weekend, I'll do it. The key is not to get sucked in.

I've also learned a new tactic to improve my ability to be present with my kids: bunnies. When the kids get home from school, they come up to my home office with their bunnies, named Snickers and Cheesecake, and we spend a few minutes together, petting the bunnies and talking. There is something about being with an animal, with a being that is so uncomplicated and in the moment, that helps you be there, too. I also happen to believe it helps the kids as much as it helps me. Grown-ups might think we're the only ones whose minds are spinning in a million different directions, but theirs are, too. And if we can work together on getting our minds in check, it will benefit all of us.

There's a lot of buzz these days about the benefits of cultivating mindfulness, and I believe it can be deeply valuable for improving your focus with your kids. Here, too, entrepreneurs have a hard time, for several reasons. For one, having a mindfulness practice in which you focus on your breath takes time, and already life feels overloaded. For another, entrepreneurs are strivers, and one of the keys of mindfulness is to be nonstriving. It's the difference between forcing yourself to lift a too-heavy barbell because "dammit, I should be able to lift this, so I'm going to!" and simply doing more reps every day, adding weight little by little while being compassionate with yourself all the while. Cultivating a mindfulness practice will, in time, make it easier to switch off the work thoughts when you're with your kids. Or mindfulness will help you simply observe the thoughts go by without really engaging with them.

Change the Culture

Both men and women need to continue fighting against the judgments and stereotypes that would have us fill set gender roles, or feel guilty if we don't. And we all need to help each other know when to call it a day at work and prioritize our families.

Just a couple of years ago, I attended a meeting that started at five p.m. and had no end time. The meeting was like a free-for-all—everyone was talking over each other and debating points in never-ending circles. The man heading the meeting just sat there, staring blankly at the group. He never tried to close the circles and move the discussion forward. As this continued to go on for over three hours, I was worried I wouldn't get to see my boys before they went to bed, and looked around the room to see if anyone else was looking at the clock every minute the way I was. There were five men in the room, and I was the only woman. I finally said, "I need to get home to be with my kids." One guy turned to me and said, "What do you mean? It's eight p.m., there's plenty of time." He didn't ask what their bedtime was or how long it took me to get home (which was an hour). I didn't feel like I could be the one to call it a day; I wasn't leading the meeting. But there was undoubtedly some gender pressure at play, too. As the only woman, I didn't want to be the one to say "enough is enough" because that might signal I wasn't committed. I should have, and I feel more empowered to do so now. But just as important, the men in the room needed to say it, too, or to back me up when I pointed out the time. It's entirely possible they wanted to get home to their families just as much as I did, but they didn't feel that, as men, they could voice that desire.

I was on another board that I loved, but that took two-day retreats that were hard on my family life. This board also had meetings that went on interminably. Although I would ask the CEO in advance when the board meetings were supposed to close and he'd give me a time, the meetings started to go later and later, way past the time they were supposed to end. I had to duck out of them so I could go home to pick up my boys, but when I mentioned that I had to leave, the board chairman said, "There really isn't an end time for these meetings. Everyone just wants to keep going." Later, after the company was sold, I asked the chairman for feedback about my contributions. He said, "Well, it would have been good if you'd stayed longer in the board meetings."

Here's the thing: holding a meeting with no apparent end time makes it challenging for busy people to manage a life. With other boards I'm on, when we manage to a time line, we get the most important and strategic issues addressed. A time line, which is so respectful for everyone present, ensures that critical things get done and that a board isn't overmanaging a company. Someone needs to be monitoring the clock and saying, "We need to move on. Should we table this particular point until the next meeting or take an action step?"

There is a shift that takes place when more women are present that's good for everyone, and I think that in each of these two examples, if there had been more women there, the dynamic—and the logistics—would have been different. It's more likely there would have been an end time to the meeting, for one. But also, when there are two women present, we encourage each other to talk. When there are three of us, it changes the whole game. There's enough mass that it creates a tipping point. The board starts thinking differently, addressing different issues, being more respectful of every person in the room. The conversations are richer, and the approaches start to leverage the best of both men and women. It used to be that this type of room was rare. But now I see changes in attitudes and can imagine a future where it's much more common.

I'm seeing hopeful changes for men, too. They may not feel as much judgment about missing their kids' activities as moms do (although some now do), but that doesn't mean they want to be working a zillion hours and missing first steps and doctor's appointments. They don't have the same physical mandate to take time off to deliver and nurse a child, but that doesn't mean they don't want to be home and participatory in such an important time. I have a friend, Robert, who, when he became a dad, received a lot of pushback for wanting to take parental leave. "That policy is really meant for women," his boss said, then added, "and won't your wife have help from her family?" Robert took the leave anyway, and took an even longer leave for his second child. Now the younger generation of men who watched him do it are taking leave, too, when they become fathers. And that is how tipping points work. Canadian prime minister Justin Trudeau earned a lot of accolades for appointing a cabinet that was 50 percent female, and even more accolades for his response to someone asking him why he did it: "Because it's 2015." He's also spoken of how in addition to encouraging his daughter's ambition, he needs to take as much effort to talk to his sons "about how he treats women and how he is going to grow up to be a feminist just like Dad." Trudeau has famously said, "We shouldn't be afraid of the word feminist. Men and women should use it to describe themselves any time they want."[*]

I hope that Prime Minister Trudeau's move is just the beginning, and that in addition to more visibility in the political sphere, more women will become entrepreneurs. Only 10 percent of startups that raised Series A funding in 2014 had female founders.[†] Of the most successful companies, those started by men began with six times as much capital as those founded by women. Not only is this unfair, but it makes no sense, since, over time, women-led companies outperform all others but blue chips.[‡] But there's hope. Crunchbase, a site that tracks data on tech companies, said that the number of startups with at least one female founder more than quadrupled between 2009 and 2014.[§] We will keep moving in a positive direction if women start seeing other women lean into entrepreneurship, and if more funding gets to these entrepreneurs.

I hope that by the time my sons are grown with families of their own, they will not blink about missing work to volunteer at their kids' elementary school, and that they'll work for employers who understand the importance of family life. (Hell, they might even *be* those employers.) When I asked

[*] Ceri Parker, "Justin Trudeau: I Will Raise My Sons as Feminists," World Economic Forum blog, January 22, 2016, www.weforum.org/agenda/2016/01/justin-trudeau-i-will-raise-my-sons-as-feminists.

[†] Lisa Calhoun, "30 Surprising Facts about Female Founders," *Inc.*, July 6, 2015.

[‡] Ibid.

[§] Ibid.

my sons the other day what they thought about the capabilities of women leaders, they both said they didn't understand my question. They said, as if it were a trick question, "What's the difference from men?" However, we still have ground to cover, and we can't become complacent.

Men are becoming a stronger and stronger voice, asking for the time they want with their kids, and they need to keep doing so. In her book *Overwhelmed*, Brigid Schulte interviewed a stay-at-home dad named Howard Kraibel, who said, "Men are starting to realize, Wow, we lose this massive dimension of our relationship with our kids by just enslaving ourselves at work all the time. . . . And we're starting to figure it out, that we need to have that connection, too."* Schulte also wrote about the increasing influence these dads have on the culture around us. "When Huggies aired a new ad showing an inept father trying to change a diaper," she wrote, "a group of very adept new dads organized a protest against the outdated stereotype until Huggies removed the ad and apologized."†

It's moments like these that make me feel strong in the prediction I voiced at the outset of the chapter: twenty years from now, a book like this won't need this chapter at all. We just need to take it one Huggies ad at a time.

---

*Brigid Schulte, *Overwhelmed: Work, Love, and Play When No One Has the Time* (New York: Farrar, Straus and Giroux, 2014), 228.

† Ibid.

CHAPTER 6

Calling You on Your Shit

The Entrepreneur and Friendship

O ne beautiful fall day, my close friend and neighbor Marissa invited me over for coffee, a pretty normal occurrence, as we tried to get together as much as we could. I'd known her for years, and one of the things I loved about her was that she was bold. She was loud, fun, and sometimes inappropriate. But it took someone with guts like that to do what she did. We were sitting on her deck that overlooked the Oakland hills, and seemingly out of the blue she said, "Allison and I are worried about you. You're losing too much weight, and I think you're on a slippery slope to anorexia."

"What? Really?" I asked, perplexed. I was psyched that my workout and eating routine was finally shedding pounds, and couldn't understand how anyone could interpret that as anorexia. More than anything, I was shocked that Marissa and Allison were worried enough to talk to each other about it, since they were really just acquaintances through me. I was surprised, but I didn't take the comment seriously. I felt that perhaps they were jealous I was losing weight, a thought I'm ashamed of now.

Not sure exactly what to say, I told Marissa, "I understand your concern and I appreciate it." I figured I would make her feel better and the subject would drop.

Then I knew I had to talk to Allison, too. Allison was a good friend I'd made at Clif Bar, an avid climber and a total character. Her opening line when she met me was, "I have to ask you, are you a bagel?" (Translation: "Are you Jewish?" Since she was, she recognized my fellow Jewishness.) Allison hadn't said a word to me about my weight, but soon after my afternoon with Marissa, we met up to watch our kids in a town Halloween parade. I brought it up. "Marissa told me that you guys talked," I said. "She said you're concerned about me."

"Yeah," she said, barely taking her eyes off the colorful parade of miniature Spider-Men, Jedis, and princesses before us. "You actually look like a Holocaust victim."

As you can see, my friends don't pull punches. I told Allison the same thing I'd told Marissa, that I was fine but also really grateful for their concern. I didn't see Allison for a long time after that, not because I was upset with her for questioning my health, but because I was too busy with Plum. And so she didn't see me start to look and act even less like myself. In fact, her comment about my looking like a Holocaust victim was made when I was about fifteen pounds over my lowest weight.

When you're wrapped up in an entrepreneurial venture, it is incredibly easy to lose your bearings and also incredibly dangerous to do so. Sometimes this obsession will lead to anorexia, drug addiction, or alcoholism—name your poison.

Having a support network can serve as a touchstone to what you value most, and being willing to listen to someone saying "You are not okay" can save your life. Friendships are crucial for the emotional well-being of an entrepreneur, but they are often the first thing to hit the chopping block when things get busy. As with many entrepreneurs, I felt I couldn't take the time out for friends, especially since I was finding it hard to be with my family. What I see now is that full immersion in a great conversation could have helped me breathe. And really hearing my friends' concerns could have forced me to address my health much earlier. At the least, it could have served as the canary in the coal mine, telling me that something wasn't right.

We can all agree that friendship gets an overall mark in the "plus" column of life, but when you are stretched so thin that something has to go, it's an easy category to discard. Your relationships with employees or investors, people whom you are surrounded by 95 percent of the time, but who also have skin in the game, are simply not the same as your relationships with your friends. The honesty level is different. The comfort level is different. The support level is different. There are scores of reasons—business and otherwise—that friendships should be savored, *especially* when there's no time. Here are my top three.

Reason 1: It's Good for Your Business

Entrepreneurs can easily become myopic, and that's never a good thing. Say you founded a kiosk that rents DVDs. Your whole world, 24/7, is focused on getting these kiosks up and running, choosing which DVDs to feature, hiring staff, and scaling up as quickly as you can. Let's say DVD kiosks have been your life for two years. You haven't seen any of your best friends in ages, and so you don't know that none of them even owns a DVD player anymore. The point is, you have to stay connected to the world outside your narrow one in order to make sure your ideas are still relevant—not according to some marketing study or other, but according to common sense.

Also, when you talk to your outside friends about what's going on in your business, they can provide an entirely new, different perspective. They don't live, breathe, and sleep the business like those working with you do. All they really have at stake is their concern for you, with no other vested interest; they're not caught in the same web you and your team are, they don't have conflicts of interest that other business partners like investors, suppliers, and vendors have. From that more distant place, not only can great ideas arise, but also great feedback about how—or if—you're changing.

Since your friends are not deep into your venture, explaining it to them forces you to simplify your message, concept, and business problems in a way that can help you and the people you work with get clear on what you're trying to accomplish. I'll always remember having dinner with my cousins who came to visit us just when Patrick and I were working on our business ideas. Patrick shared the concept of Blue Sky so simply: "It's the place you always wanted to take your kids, where there are creative and physical activities with healthy food—the anti–Chuck E. Cheese's." The cousins cheered him on. "What a great idea, Patrick! That's a killer concept—so needed." Although Blue Sky didn't work, he explained it so clearly and crisply. He had nailed the need (and that need still needs filling; our challenge was execution). Then I explained

Plum as this collective of organic, healthy brands where you'd get the efficiencies of scale. "Oh, okay," they responded. They didn't get it. I realized that we really needed to get much clearer on what the consumer need was that we were intending to fulfill. I needed to grasp, too, how to sell it. And, once Neil and I really got that clarity, we were able to sell the vision to anyone.

Talking about your business with friends is important, but you have to know when it's time to just shut up about it and talk about anything else. Remember that although your work may seem endlessly interesting to you, it's usually less than half as interesting to others, even if they're in a similar industry. Your friends will remind you of that, or you won't have any in the long run. When I left Plum, Allison and I were talking, and the discussion started veering back to work. I turned to her and said, "Can we just be together and talk about other things so we can forget about work for a while?" She was down with that. Two years later, we were at a restaurant eating dinner with our husbands, and when I asked her about work, she said, "Can we just not talk about it? I loved when you suggested that. I just want to immerse myself with being with you guys." Those conversations have now given us a language to use to be able to put work in its place and make friendship the center of our attention. Our work is important in our friendships; just not all the time.

Reason 2: It Helps Maintain Your Full Identity

You are not your startup. There were lots of years of life before you started your company, and there will be years after you have left your company, or your company has left you. But at the point when your work occupies a dispropor-tionate amount of your time and energy, it's easy to lose sight of the fact that you actually have multiple dimensions and that people knew you—and know you—as someone com-pletely divorced from your business role. Keep in touch with those people, and you will keep in touch with your fuller self. Remember in high school when you blew off all your friends because of your obsession with your boyfriend? This is like the grown-up version of that. But you know better now—or, that is, you should.

After I left Plum, I was depressed and forgot how to smile. I remember sitting in a closet in the basement of my parents' home in Michigan, looking through old photos, letters, and mementos. As I was sorting through the cards, I found one from Sue, a friend of mine from my undergraduate years, whom I'd lost touch with long ago. In her card, she thanked me for helping her find a new group of friends who helped her get out of the superficial world that she'd been a part of in high school. She wrote that my energy and enthusi-asm helped her feel deeply cared for and appreciated. Tears started to run down my cheeks, as this friendship from so long ago reminded me of how I usually related to the world, and what I had lost as I mourned Plum. It was as if my friend Sue was with me at that moment, reminding me of the person I wanted to become again.

The peace with yourself that comes from deep friendships reaches, in my case, to my extended family, those who don't just live in my house day in and day out. In October 2015, I was slammed at REBBL. We were in the thick of fund-raising, still initiating new investor conversations while trying to nurture other relationships we hoped might become serious investors. (For perspective, in the search process, I spoke with over fifty investors, of which twenty-one were second-level or deeper conversations. I also was keeping up to date the forty-five angel investors who were already invested in our company.) Patrick and I had plans to attend my cousin's wedding in Ohio, and I seriously thought about canceling. It would be a whirlwind trip—we'd be there only twenty-four hours, and the rest would be travel. We'd have to leave the kids at home, since they had school on Monday, and I'd have to miss a day of work. I had just seen this extended family the previous year, and I was seeing my parents and brother again the next month in Michigan for Thanksgiving. I just generally dreaded going. (What a whiner I am, right?) I even thought about "calling in sick," but every time I considered cancel-ing, I thought about how it would make the bride and groom feel, and also about how this trip might be my last chance to see my beloved uncle Gary, the older brother of my dad who passed away when I was very young. Uncle Gary was ailing. My relationship with my dad's brothers, Gary and Ken, was such an important connection to my dad, so the prospect of losing my uncle deeply saddened me. I knew I'd always regret not going if he passed away before I could see him again. We live across the country from most of our family—it's not like I could pop by with a pot of soup when it was convenient for me and hold his hand. Seeing family took effort, but maybe that was a good thing. In this way, it felt like my love for my uncle was forcing me out of complete immersion in REBBL.

The trip was in fact busy and exhausting, but I'm so happy that I went. We got to sit at the "cousins" table with relatives who were on average about twenty or thirty years younger than Patrick and me. I had lived far away from them for so long that I just knew them as "the kids," so it was meaning-ful to connect with them and hear about their budding rela-tionships, their engaging careers, their dreams for the future. I also got to connect with my aunt Ellyse and uncle Kenny, who are such upbeat, smiley people, it makes me happy being around them. We spent some time with my brother and sister-in-law, Steve and Geri, and my parents, drinking wine and planning our next meal together. (That always seems to happen with family. While you're eating, you're always plan-ning the next meal.) Seeing my uncle Gary was meaningful, but so was the act of my going at all. That act meant that I was living in accordance with my values, and my values were a lot broader reaching than what was going on at REBBL. When I went back to work the next week, I felt more sane and less critical of myself. In ways that surprised me, traveling halfway across the country to be a wedding guest was just an incred-ibly grounding thing to do. My uncle Gary ended up passing away five months later, and I was so grateful to have gone to the wedding, where I'd hugged him and told him that I loved him.

Being a friend or a family member forces you to take on that identity. You can't just take in the relationship; you have to give, too. Valuing these relationships reminds you that it's not in fact all about you. Being a friend offers a buffer against narcissism and obsession. Remember that the intensity that entrepreneurs are so susceptible to must be guarded against so that it doesn't become destructive. If you've been spinning all day long about a decision, just sitting with someone else and offering your attention and care to them can pull you out of that dangerous headspace.

When I was grinding at work, I wasn't always great at seeing my friends. Thank god these friends didn't desert me, but rather they were there when I realized my error. How could I not have taken a moment to be with them? I'm adamant about making sure that every time I part with a friend, we put another date on the calendar that very moment. Patrick and I literally book three months in advance with people just to make sure that we have a plan to see them again. People think it's silly at first, but you wouldn't believe how fast that date comes up again. The other thing I'm a firm believer in is the value of a phone call. Even if you feel slammed, you can take a fifteen-minute walk and call a friend while you're walking. Fifteen minutes can be unbelievably grounding.

Reason 3: It Helps Heal You (and Them)

There are dozens of studies that show that friendships are good for our health, and that they have been associated with longer survival rates from cancers, greater longevity, and re-duced incidents of dementia. There's also some research that suggests that we release stress-reducing hormones when we care for others or are being cared for. An article published by Harvard Health Publications argued that social connections "influence our long-term health in ways every bit as powerful as adequate sleep, a good diet, and not smoking."[*]

When Patrick was at his lowest, one of the best things he did for his health was to confide in Marissa, who was not only my friend but his as well. In the aftermath of Blue Sky, the

---

[*] "The Health Benefits of Strong Relationships," *Harvard Women's Health Watch*, December 2010, www.health.harvard.edu/newsletter_article/the-health -benefits-of-strong-relationships.

emotional fallout hit him intensely. He was depressed about causing a financial crisis in our family, for having to lay off employees, and about the public nature of how quickly what he'd called "the Taj Mahal" had to close. He felt like a failure, that he'd let us down, that he'd let down people who had counted on him. The two of us talked constantly, of course, but I was part of what he felt bad about. So he kept a lot inside, and it caused insomnia and anxiety. We were talking about it recently, and he said, "I was so not where I wanted to be in my life. It was all I could think about. I had that feeling that *I do not want to be here. And there is no shortcut out of this space.*" He hadn't planned to open up to Marissa, but he ran into her while he was picking up the kids at school. She asked, "How are you holding up?" and the words spilled out of him like water charging through a broken dam. He told her how lousy he felt, how stressed he was, how hard it was to sleep, and how there were no easy solutions in sight and that he was obsessively thinking about it. They spoke for only about five or ten minutes, but he told me how good it felt to share it with someone. Marissa felt grateful that he was willing to open up and share his feelings. It also opened up the opportunity for them to talk about it in the future instead of feeling like they would be walking on eggshells around the topic when they saw each other again. The connection was positive for both of them, in the way healthy two-way-street friendships are. "This is going to make a good story one day!" Marissa said. Although Patrick felt at that moment that he never wanted it to be a story, period, it did offer him a glimpse out of the space in time that he felt would never end. Talking to a friend didn't cure Patrick of his unhappiness, but it was an important start, and one that allowed him to open up to other people and say he was feeling bad.

The point of this all is very clear: choose a friend you trust, and open up to him or her. Write down a list of your greatest fears with your business and share them. This is a task that's easier for women, it must be said. I could tiptoe around making stereotypes, but we all know that on the whole, women tend to form strong friendships, they put more effort into keeping in touch, they nurture their friends and accept nurturing in return. It's not that men aren't capable of this, but they've been conditioned to be more stoic and to never show weakness, and they often don't have the networks of friends that women do. This is an area where men could really stand to learn from the women entrepreneurs in their lives. See where these women are getting support, and ask for nothing less for yourself.

Know *Real* Friendship

Friendship is sometimes hanging out watching a game together, but that's really more companionship than anything else. And so beware the friends who overlook changes in your health or personality and focus instead on your achievements. Are they reinforcing your bad habits, or are they calling you on your shit?

James Eisenberg gained eighty pounds during the years he worked in Silicon Valley. "I would get up at six and work until two in the morning," he said. "I ate out twenty-one meals a week, and half of those meals were business meetings. I was totally unhealthy." He was at the top of his game in many ways, and on track to be a venture capital–funded CEO. But he chose to leave, and he thinks that if he'd stayed he'd have had a massive heart attack within five years. James feels leaving was a great decision, but it wasn't one his friends understood at all. "They thought I was insane when I left," he said. "They couldn't believe it. The things that you get congratulated on, they have no idea that you're rotting from the inside. If you're driving an Aston Martin and last year you were driving a Mercedes, they don't care that your life is in turmoil. It's a powerful drug. People don't tell you to get out. Most of them are striving for what you've got. They're climbing a ladder and they have no idea what's at the top."

Real friends would have said, "Hey, man, are you taking care of yourself?" I am so grateful my friends asked me this question, even if it took me a while to hear it. Allison and Marissa started the drumbeat, and Neil said something early on, too. Then my friend Deb, whom I'd become close with through my Vistage CEO group, called and asked if she could come see me. I thought it was unusual, because typically Deb and I got together as part of the foursome group of Vistage alums. As we sat down for lunch, she held my hand and said, "We're worried about you." That registered. It was only a tiny bit, but it registered. The feedback now wasn't just a few data dots; it was actually making a line. I was coming to recognize that line for what it was. Then in April 2014, my four best friends who had been bridesmaids in my wedding came to visit for the weekend. My friend Anj was the first to arrive. She flew in from Brooklyn, and I hadn't seen her in a while. As I opened the door to give her a hug, she stared at me with a look of horror on her face. "What happened, Sheryl? You're way too skinny. Something is wrong."

"I'm aware," I said. We sat down and I just shared everything. How hard it had all been: Blue Sky, Plum, and how I just kept it inside. As the rest of my friends showed up, the weekend was filled with lots of love as well as challenging conversations. That weekend was the final impetus to get me to open up and write this book so that others could know they aren't alone.

My friends still hold me accountable for my health. Several, including one, Danae, whom I have known for over twenty-five years, check in all the time about my weight, and I'm really clear that I need to spend time alone with them so we can really talk. Over time, it's been great to have them say, "You look better." I can't hide. Nor would I ever want to.

If you are putting your friendships in the background, if you consider them an indulgence rather than a necessity, stop. They are the ones to say, "Hey, it's not normal to sit in front of a screen for as many hours as you do," or "Did you know that you don't smile anymore?" or "You're drinking a lot more than you ever used to—what's going on?" or "You don't seem like yourself. You are talking a mile a minute and don't seem able to sit still. What's up?" or "You are not looking well—you have huge circles under your eyes. Are you sleeping? Do you feel okay? We are worried about you." In other words, they'll call you on your shit like no one else can—and it may save your life.

Part II

DOING THE WORK

In part II, I make the case that *you* are the most valuable resource to your company. If you use yourself up climbing your way to the top, then all the profit and acclaim in the world will be worthless once you get there. A sick day, a breather, a tropical beach vacation is not going to kill you or your company—but a heart attack or a nervous breakdown just might kill both. I came close to losing my footing because I put taking care of everyone and everything else above taking care of myself. I was terrified of looking like I couldn't handle it, like I wasn't fully on top of it all. My self-worth was so wrapped up in Plum that, in hindsight, I can see that I didn't get the support I needed, from the beginning, before a problem had the possibility of arising. We need to use the precautionary principle as entrepreneurs and take care of ourselves, for the good of our companies and all our stakeholders.

CHAPTER 7

Climbing High

The Entrepreneur and Risk

M y coinstructor at Sonoma State, Professor Armand Gilinsky, plays a game with budding entrepreneurs. On
the first night of class, he says, "Here I have twenty-
five dollars that I'll give you right now, or you can bet on the
come, and be willing to wait until the last class, when I'll give
you a hundred dollars. I might not show up to the last class,
or I might show up but not have the money. Or *you* might not
show up." One student volunteers and takes the twenty-five
dollars that night, and another waits.

At the end of the course, Armand asks the class which of
the two students is the entrepreneur and which is the venture
capitalist. Distinguishing between the two roles is important
for helping students understand their assumptions about risk.
Most initially assume that of the two roles, the entrepreneur
takes the greater risks, while the venture capitalist sits back
and watches. On the first night of class, most students peg
the one who waited for the hundred dollars as the entrepreneur, but by the last night, they know better. "They realize

that the entrepreneur always takes the sure money," Armand said, "and the venture capitalist is willing to be somewhat patient, deal with uncertainty, and hope that the waiting will bring a higher valuation for the company. So their whole conception of entrepreneurs as risk takers is exploded." A skilled entrepreneur, in other words, is the one who will assign risk to *somebody else*. The entrepreneur will take the resources when they're there. She is always looking to risk-reduce the business as she drives rapid innovation.

Many people think entrepreneurship is about taking risks. "Be bold! Go all in!" There's a macho all-or-nothing mentality about risks in business. You've seen the headlines: "He risked it all . . . and came out on top!" Or "Gambling on success—and winning!" Well, the truth about entrepreneurs and risk is much less exciting, and its lessons leave more lasting impressions than a headline can.

To play the game at all, of course, you have to be somewhat of a risk taker. It feels much safer to work for someone else, where you expect that you'll have a steady paycheck and that the doors won't be in danger of closing the next day because of a decision you've made. Under the umbrella of a big company, you can pull a lever and know that certain things will likely happen. There are masses of data, and departmental checks on risk, to make everything safer. It's not like that at startups—there are no levers, no departments, and there is no certainty. So of course starting a business is inherently risky, just as we can all agree mountain climbing is inherently risky. But here's the thing: Would you go climbing without the proper gear? Probably not, and you shouldn't approach business any differently. Entrepreneurship is about *minimizing* risk.

Minimizing risk, or assigning it to someone else, is not the equivalent of being fearful, yet so many people equate the two. Entrepreneurs can't be too fearful, for fear is what holds you back from being bold. But being bold and taking outsize risks are also not the same thing. There is a very important difference. Being bold means you go climbing; taking an *outsize* risk means you leave the safety gear at home.

Love and Ego: The Perpetrators of Outsize Risk

There are two central culprits that can muddy your vision so that you can't see the difference between being bold and taking unreasonable risks: love and ego.

We already covered some of the downsides of love in chapter 1. Love for your endeavor can make you blind and deaf to sirens screaming, "Stop! Or for god's sake, at least slow down!" I know that Patrick and I suffered from this. We were so in love with the idea of Blue Sky that we didn't seek enough information. As Patrick says now, if he had shadowed someone in the field for even a single day, he would have seen it was much harder than we expected, and not as fun. But we wanted so badly to believe, we wanted so badly to make it happen. We didn't look at our risks realistically, because we were blinded by our love of our concept and what we thought it might mean to families in our community. We imagined how fun it would be for our friends to come to Blue Sky for the day. Our kids would run around together while the adults would drink beer, eat some good, healthy food, and laugh while someone else dealt with the kid chaos.

After we signed the paperwork at the bank to take on the loan, we smiled huge smiles and took selfies of ourselves with the check in hand. It makes my stomach turn to think about how, in that instant, we handed all our savings to the Gods of Risk, who were lying in wait to show us one big-ass life lesson. But we were blind to them.

Imagine the mountain climber who's head-over-heels in love with the sport. Mt. Everest is all he talks about—it's all he's talked about for years. He's determined to reach the summit, which he sees as the pinnacle of his climbing career. He can see himself on top, surveying the world around him, basking in the dramatic landscape and the knowledge that he has done it. This climber is driven by passion and grit. And he might also be very dangerous to go climbing with. Does this mountain climber have the wherewithal to turn back when he's close to the summit because of a dark weather forecast? Is he able to make that call with a clear enough head so that he doesn't take outsize risks? And let's say he knows he should bring extra oxygen and extra emergency supplies, but he also knows the added weight will slow him down and lower his chances of summiting. Can he make the right choice to mitigate his risk? The question isn't rhetorical, and in fact a scenario very similar to this one led to the Everest disaster in 1996, in which eight people died.

There are plenty of great climbers who love the sport and also make risk-minimizing choices. And usually those choices involve turning around, even when it's hard to do so, knowing that they can go back and try again another day.

Stimson Bullitt was a prominent lawyer and activist who pursued his passion for climbing well into his eighties. In his posthumously published book *Illusion Dweller*, he wrote about the outdoorsman whose judgment and self-discipline are compromised for the desire for just "one big climb."

Their competitive motive may be as much external as internal," he wrote. "That is, they are competing for the approval of non-climbers. They have climbed little and expect to climb little more, but seek one big score with which to notch their belts. They often take substantial risks because they do not calibrate risk with the precision that experience brings. Their longing to make the summit suppresses their prudence, which may be telling them to turn back even though they are so near their goal. Such a person, having gotten himself to 20,000 feet, may be hard to deter from tottering and gasping on, even in the face of his declining condition and that of his surroundings, both of which indicate low survival odds.°

I cannot read those words without thinking of entrepreneurs and the ways they have their sights trained on one spot and one spot only. The big E, ego, is of course intertwined with all of this. An entrepreneur has to accept that most ventures *won't* be financially successful—period. You can't make the mistake of thinking you'll beat the odds just because you have a fancy degree, stellar experience, and great contacts. The statistics do in fact apply to you, too. It's an incredibly tricky line to walk, because as an entrepreneur, you do need to be bold, to have vision, to see what isn't there and believe that it can be built. But you must be careful that you don't cross over into reality distortion, in which you willfully deny what's right in front of you.

Dr. Michael Freeman is a psychiatrist and researcher who

°Stimson Bullitt, *Illusion Dweller: The Climbing Life of Stimson Bullitt* (Seattle: Mountaineers Books, 2013), 136.

is also an executive coach and an entrepreneur himself. He's also the lead researcher on one of the only studies done about the mental health of entrepreneurs. "I think a lot of entrepreneurs have a distorted perspective about the nature of the work that they're undertaking," he said. "They have an optimistic bias. The way that works is that everybody knows going into it that four out of five startups fail within the first five years. So if you ask any entrepreneur, they'll tell you that they are aware of this, but they'll also tell you 'I'm the one in five that's going to make it.'" They'll give reasons for this, he said. They'll explain that they're an expert on the Lean Startup, or that they have the right relationships, or some proprietary technology, or a killer team. "What's left out of that," Dr. Freeman explained, "is that businesses fail for reasons that have nothing to do with the founder."

So what happens when this optimistic bias takes a fall, or threatens to? It's not pretty.

When Patrick founded Blue Sky, we decided that he wouldn't take on investors, since I already had investors at Plum. We would be the sole owners. We thought we were minimizing risk, because I'd traded equity in Plum for a salary. By keeping control of Blue Sky and Patrick not getting a salary, we stood to gain more. So in many ways, we felt we were hedging our bets. We also knew that getting investors would mean ceding control, and we didn't want that—we wanted to be fully in charge. Full of our optimistic bias, we felt confident that Blue Sky would succeed. It was a great concept, and between both of our MBAs from top universities and forty years of combined business experience, we thought we could beat the odds. We took on much more risk than our family should have. Though a restaurant entrepreneur warned us not to risk more than 10 percent of our wealth, we didn't listen. That seems crazy now, but you have to keep the context in mind. As a budding entrepreneur, you hear from *everyone* about what's wrong with your idea, and everyone has an opinion. "That idea is too out there." "You won't raise money." "Your financial projections are too rosy"—and on and on. You also hear the advice to "Go for it!" "An entrepreneur can never veer from her vision," people say. "No one believed in Steve Jobs, and look what he did; he just shot from his gut and never looked back." We started buying into the optimistic story and shook off the bad stuff as "the naysayers and doubters." We could do this!

At first, it was a total adrenaline rush, creating the look and feel of our play space, and watching the walls go up, the paint go on, and the vision turn into a reality. Then the obstacles began. Due to issues that emerged from needing to pass strict building codes, Blue Sky's opening was delayed. Given unplanned upgrades required by the city and our paying rent with no revenue to offset the cost, we spent more than we had planned for or expected. Blue Sky finally opened in September 2008, but then for the next two months the weather was perfect—a killer for an indoor play space.

Just six short months after the day we took those grinning selfies with the loan check, one otherwise sunny day Patrick came home speechless, white as a ghost, and cold to the touch. He told me that we'd run through all our cash. At first, I didn't believe it could be possible. And after all this effort, how could we just let it go? So we dipped into our 401(k), thinking that would give us enough time to attract more members. We lost all our savings and almost went personally bankrupt. We spoke with a bankruptcy attorney, who told us that we'd lose everything of value in our house and, of course, the house itself. So we sold the house as fast as we could and moved into the top half of a rental home. The landlord, who lived downstairs, had a yappy white lapdog named Poppy. We all thought Poppy was adorable, until we learned that when we heard the dog coming up the stairs, it meant the landlady was coming, too. She would chew us out for every infraction—the kids making too much noise, too much clutter, too much . . . too much. She was right—it was all too much.

The death knell hit right before Christmas break. Patrick and I were walking around in a state of shock and dismay. We felt like we were playing Whack-a-Mole. Once we thought we had one problem solved, another one would pop up. Some former Blue Sky club members demanded their money back. We felt terrible that we had let them down, and deeply embarrassed, so we paid everyone out of our personal checking account when we were down to our last cent. We were sued by a company that claimed we'd given a personal guarantee. In that case, we hadn't, and we pushed them hard to produce the paperwork, which they never could. But we had to go to court to see it through. The Blue Sky building landlord wouldn't let us out of our hefty rent, even though at the end of the day we'd done wonders with his dumpy building, including updating the kitchen, sprinkler system, bathrooms, HVAC, and fire escape to bring it up to code. Then there was the Small Business Administration loan we'd gotten through the bank that we were trying to negotiate down, since we were doing everything we could to avoid bankruptcy. We started getting calls from credit card companies, from the company that installed our security—everyone wanted their money, and we had none left. We were petrified and trying to hold it together for our kids and for each other.

We knew we couldn't pace the house like zombies over the holiday, but we couldn't stomach seeing anyone. At the last minute, we gathered up the boys and drove to a two-hundred-square-foot rental cabin in the woods of Humboldt County. The cabin was surrounded by giant redwoods that disappeared into the clouds. There was no one else around for miles. We sat together for four days in that cabin, knee to knee, playing board games and eating homemade chili. Every so often, we'd go out mushroom hunting in the frosty air. My greatest recollections of that weekend involve squeezing my kids, watching them sleep, and staring at the frost on the earth while trying to do everything I could to ground myself and remember what was really important. We found peace in that nature sanctuary. But both Patrick and I just couldn't stomach the thought of going back to the post–Blue Sky hell.

There is so much in hindsight that we should have done differently to mitigate our risk. Though Patrick and I knew consumer products inside and out, we didn't know the recreation and restaurant business. Of the many lessons we learned, here are a few:

1. We should have talked to more people, which would have helped us understand that you *never* start paying a lease until you have people coming through the door. You push the landlord hard to make the upgrades needed to pass city inspection.

2. We could have taken on a cofounder who was an expert in recreation and restaurants, and not have been so set on controlling it 100 percent ourselves.

3. Patrick could have worked at a similar business—even a Chuck E. Cheese's!—to understand the dynamics of the business and see if he really loved it, or we could have hooked up with an existing business.

Near the end of Blue Sky, Patrick reached out to a competitor in another city close by to look at our business. Although most entrepreneurs hide what they think are their secrets, we learned a great lesson in getting help from wherever you can. The competitor instantly saw what was wrong with the business—we had too big of a menu, for one. He also noted we had no video games, which really produce the profit (although we were trying to avoid having video games, it would have helped to have known their impact, so we would have better understood our choice). He said Patrick could have joined with him as a partner on his business, but it was too late. The damage was done because the commitments were made and the money was spent.

4. We could have bought an existing business that had a stable source of revenue and made upgrades over time, after testing them in the market. We could have even held out until we got an angel investor who had "patient capital" (i.e., an investor who didn't want a fast payout). Nowadays we could have raised money through a crowdfunding site like Kickstarter or Indiegogo.

There are so many ways to learn before investing in something of this magnitude. Patrick was less humble at that point in his life, and so was I. We simply thought our skills were more transferable than they were, and that the power of our love for our idea could see us through anything.

It's difficult to read the temperature of your own ego-love thermometer, as our story shows. You can start by asking some tough questions of yourself and answering them honestly. Have you done your research thoroughly? That means talking to as many people in the business as you can, even the ones you'd guess are naysayers. If you haven't done the research, why? Is it because you don't want to hear what it has to say? How have you reacted when people have spoken negatively about your concept? Are you able to be open and analytical about their feedback? Are you using "exception" language, as in "Yeah, I know the odds are long, but . . ." or "I'm sure this will work despite that because . . ." If you talk to enough people (Steve Blank recommends as many as possible, and try for at least a hundred), are you finding a thread of truth in the comments?

Have you done some experimentation with your concept to see, quantitatively, how people react to the idea, the price, your marketing messages? Thanks to the Internet, it's cheap to do this kind of testing. See how consumers respond by seeing what they actually do in real life in the market. Experiment your way into whether or not your product will be successful and how to pivot it if it's not. In Blue Sky's case, we could have created a Web landing page announcing a new play space and seen how many people entered, where they went in the virtual play space, how many times they'd pay. Test, test, test. If you find a model that seems to work, don't immediately take a huge plunge, but instead start building it more. Step by step, reduce the risk the way a scientist proves a hypothesis. In a report that analyzed 3,200 high-growth Web/mobile startups, 92 percent of them failed, and 74 percent of those failed due to premature scaling.* The lesson in that is clear: slow down! Hypothesize, test, measure, learn, revise, repeat.

The one risk we didn't take on Blue Sky was our love for each other. Connor was nine years old when everything was falling apart. He brought his piggy bank downstairs, reached inside, and pulled out fifty cents. "Here, Daddy," he said as he handed it to Patrick. "I'll be an investor in Blue Sky." We never stopped believing in each other no matter how hard it got. We were in it together and we would get through it and over it together.

Risk and Self-Awareness

When you feel you've cleared all the muck away so that you can see the risk clearly, there's something else you need to do: you need to look at *yourself* clearly. We've established that if you are an entrepreneur or want to be one, you have *some* measure of comfort with risk. But what is that comfort level? And why does it matter?

It's important to really know your comfort level with risk simply because if you push yourself too much and things don't go according to the plan (which is a sure bet, by the way), you will fall far. Think sleepless nights, drinking too much, losing your temper, pushing the people away whom you need, ulcers, drugs—anything to numb the pain.

*Quora.com Startup Genome Report Extra on Premature Scaling, a project coauthored by Berkeley and Stanford faculty members with Steve Blank and ten startup accelerators as contributors. https://s3.amazonaws.com/startup compass-public/StartupGenomeReport2_Why_Startups_Fail_v2.pdf.

Pattie Sellers, a longtime *Fortune* editor and founder of *Fortune*'s Most Powerful Women (MPW) Summit, recently went part-time at *Fortune* to start SellersEaston Media with her colleague Nina Easton. Leaving a comfortable perch that she had held for decades was daunting, so she took the leap and kept a foot at *Fortune* by continuing to oversee the MPW Summits. This was a way to mitigate risk, a way she could feel confident taking the plunge without fearing she'd go under.

I have a friend, Michael, who was a plaintiff's attorney before he retired. He was a sole practitioner in the area of medical malpractice and was highly respected in his field. He didn't charge his clients by the hour, but took a percentage of the settlement if his client prevailed. What this meant was that he could spend months of unpaid time, and invest thousands of dollars of his own money to pay expert witnesses, only to get nothing if the defendant didn't settle, or a jury came back in favor of the defendant. He *managed* risk, in the sense that he had a good sense of the odds based on his experience, but there are no guarantees in litigation.

Michael supported his family and financed his cases from a line of credit, not knowing when or if he'd win a favorable judgment. He'd sometimes owe the bank as much as a quarter of a million dollars, and then lose a case he thought was a sure thing. To ease his concerns, he kept a notecard in his pocket with a list of all his active cases, and when they would likely settle or go to trial. But that's all he had for reassurance—a notecard. His attorney friends told him openly that they couldn't live that way, that the uncertainty would drive them nuts. So why did he do it? He can't answer that except to say that it was his personality. "I first tried it out because I had higher financial expectations for myself than I could get at a district attorney's office, and I didn't want the hours and obligations required at a firm," he said. "But if I'd learned I couldn't stomach it, I would have done something else. As it turned out, I could handle it. I don't know why—maybe it's that I'm good at seeing the big picture and ignoring the details. Maybe I'm an optimist." I would theorize that Michael is a very smart risk mitigator, and that he also has a healthy emotional equilibrium. There might be four out of five lawyers who could manage the financial and logistical elements of the risk just as well, but not the emotional elements of it.

You need to know what your comfort level with risk is, and let that guide the multitude of choices you make every day, and inform how far it's wise for you to push the proverbial envelope. Lauren Belden of the wine label Belden Barns said she is much more prone to worry about money than her husband and cofounder, Nate. "You look at the costs," she said, "and think, Can I afford to start this business and live the lifestyle I want? There are areas I can cut back—I don't need to go to restaurants or stay at fancy places—but I don't want to leave our kids with having to pick up the pieces of our business." And so in order to launch Belden Barns, Lauren knew she needed that safety net of savings, and that for her own comfort level, she needs to keep it. "I'm terrified of fighting over money or of not being able to send our kids to college," she said. "We're at a point right now where we're fine, but my fear is that we're blowing through our life savings. But when I start to go down that hole, Nate is always quick to calm me down." Nate is the numbers side of the business, and so while Lauren will panic about how much they're spending on lawyers or on their tasting room, he can reassure her with the budget. He'll point to it and remind her that if they get below a certain number, they'll stop. The bottom won't fall out, in other words, because they've done the work to figure out how not to let the bottom fall out. And they placed their "exit" button at a number where Lauren feels comfortable. I love this plan. Similarly, we used to tell students at Stanford to have a plan for how long they should take to work on their idea. We'd tell them to give themselves a deadline and some milestones along the way. If they got to the deadline with no evidence that there was a "there there," they'd know it might be time to shut it down or pivot in a big way.

The business goals that Neil and I had at Plum were way too expensive to fund ourselves, especially because of the need to build inventory. We raised money in increments along the way. Although it was painful at times, we pinched every penny to make sure we could test and prove that we were on the right track. Sometimes we underinvested, didn't hire enough or the right people, and were quickly in over our heads. Other times, we built inventory fast enough to keep up with the business but not with our cash. It took us almost running of cash, with investors screaming down our necks, to really get how cash was truly king. But we always knew if the bottom fell out, we wouldn't lose our homes due to Plum.

Risk and the Big Picture

Adam Lowry, one of the cofounders of Method Products Inc., funded the company through his and his cofounders' own means, which were minimal. He was one of the first people I spoke with when Patrick and I were working our way out of Blue Sky. "How were you able to take that risk?" I asked him. He shrugged. "We were at the point in our lives where we could dirtbag it on the floor of a stripped-down, dumpy apartment. We only had responsibility for ourselves. We could take a lot of risk."

Many aspiring entrepreneurs would hear Adam's story—and others like his—and think, "Okay! He's saying I just need to go for it!" But that's not what he's saying at all. Rather, you have to look around you—at your life, at your responsibilities—and decide what would work. Can you really dirtbag it on the floor of a fleabag apartment with your kids, or even by yourself? Will you be okay if your business doesn't succeed financially? Will your family be?

Though Michael, the malpractice attorney, was the sole support for his family, in time he lost the stamina for litigation. He retired much sooner than he might have because the risk burned him out; he was tired of the volatility. And now he's much more conservative financially. At the risk of sounding terribly morbid, he has less time to recover if he takes a hit. It's like the stock market—you can put more on the line when you're betting that the market will balance out over time.

Your risk self-assessment might take some trial and error to pin down, but there are questions you can ask straightaway. What would you choose on Armand's twenty-five-dollars-now versus one-hundred-dollars-later test? Why? If you need to invest any earnings back into the company, instead of into your bank account, how will that feel? How much money are you willing to lose? Can you be patient enough with your idea to learn if it's right before jumping in? Is it more important to you to control your destiny, even if it means more risk, or to bring in investors who can help you grow more quickly and share the risk, but at the cost of sharing the steering wheel? What kinds of things cause you to lose sleep? Does anything? Also—and this is critical—how do you feel about plan B?

Plan B Thinking

All entrepreneurs calculating their risk have to spend time really envisioning what they'll do if their payday doesn't come. Because again, most of the time, it doesn't. Really think about it. Will your life be okay? Will your self-esteem be? Will your finances be? Again, this is something Patrick and I passed over more quickly than we should have. We didn't ask, "But what if Blue Sky falls apart quickly? What happens if we owe this bank money? What if we have a big lease we're stuck with?" It's easy to shrug questions like these off by saying you'll negotiate your way out, but what happens if you don't? Later Patrick said, "I thought I could figure some other business to create with the space if Blue Sky didn't work. But you can't just change your idea. You need to reconfigure the space, which costs more money that we didn't have. We were stuck with it."

Technically speaking, the sky did not fall and life did not come apart at the seams because Blue Sky failed. Patrick and I are still married, our relationship is stronger than ever, our kids are doing great, and our finances are back on track. We did find a way to pay the bank back over time, especially because I was making a salary and then Patrick started working at The Clorox Company. We were able to negotiate paying the equivalent of seven months of rent in one lump sum in order to get out of our lease. But it was a slow, painful recovery. The prospect of money loss, once so airy and hypothetical, became so very real. What kills me the most about what we went through was that it was so avoidable. While we did ask hard questions at the outset, and I grilled Patrick about the financial scenarios, what we didn't ask was "What happens if it bombs?" Had we just asked ourselves the *right* questions, talked to more people, and thought about what our plan B was, we would have seen that we were getting in way over our heads. Particularly when it pertains to a venture you are doing with a spouse or other family member, I can't overemphasize the importance of understanding what you're doing together, and the possible implications of that if it doesn't work.

My friend Sam was just out of business school when he started his tech company and didn't have kids or a mortgage to pay. But he did have a wife, and he warned her constantly that he might not ever make any money from the startup. If he didn't, no big deal—they didn't have anything to lose. And Sam had a lot to gain—he was building up his expertise and could use his experience at the startup to segue into a leadership role, even if the company never turned a profit. That's a pretty good plan B.

Michael had a plan B, too—several, actually. If one case didn't work out, he knew where the next one was coming from. And if case after case after case resulted in a loss, or the pressure became too much, he could leave his practice and get a job at a firm. His experience was impressive and his contacts deep. He always knew he was ultimately very employable if it came down to it.

Ask yourself how you'll feel if you fall short of your goal. Are you cool with your plan B? In *Rising Strong*, Brené Brown talks about setting the right expectations. Disappointment and shame come from setting up expectations and then being devastated when they don't work out. Brown compares it to going home on family holidays when you know the dynamic is difficult. Yet still you think, "This year it will be better." Then, when it isn't, you're deeply disappointed. Instead, do the best you can with what's there, but don't expect that someone else will change.

So how does this all apply to entrepreneurship? I'm not trying to steer you away from setting big goals. Set them. But don't believe that you will undoubtedly reach them. For instance, at REBBL we have a big goal for what we want the gross margin to be at the end of the year. It's broken down into milestones, smaller goals that we will need to hit each quarter and everything that needs to be done in order to get there. Still, at the end of the day, it's a goal that will be really hard to reach, and I'm fully aware that we might not get there. I had an open discussion with several of my board members about my concerns, making clear I really want to hit our target and will push to make it happen, but that it would be tough. The board was supportive, and one member said, "As long as you're showing a path to getting to the right direction, over time that's what's going to be the most important to outside investors and the business."

No matter what happens, our company life doesn't end on December 31, although we're trained to think that way by the financial markets. It's important to play the long game, to move in the right direction always, but to utilize plan B when needed instead of making bad choices for the company by obsessively pursuing one goal. For your company, it is critical to determine your three to five key performance indicators (KPIs), which include not only revenue and profit but things like societal impact, or employee happiness. These are the milestones for your team to pursue to accomplish the dreams you have for your business. As the leader, you have the responsibility of focusing on what the healthy balance is among all those things, depending on the stage of your business. These KPIs should also be motivating and meaningful for people, so they feel that their contributions are making a difference toward your purpose as a company. Living and dying by December 31 doesn't allow you to make great choices. For instance, with our gross margin, we can easily make our financial goal by using nonorganic ingredients and skimping on quality. But that would undermine our "quality" performance indicator. You need to find the proper balance, and you need a board that understands and supports that balance. This is what effective goal setting is all about. It means stretching, but also knowing what the upsides and downsides are and managing the path to get there.

Imagine again that mountain climber. So he didn't summit Everest. What now? Does he go home defeated? Or does he go home invigorated by the journey? He alone decides where to focus that energy. And if he says to himself, "I only have a finite amount of time to live on this planet, and look at the amazing adventure I experienced!"—then he'll be okay. He has his risk managed, and I'd go climbing with him any day.

Builders and Denters

Understanding your risk tolerance is important for your *self*, but it's also important because it affects how you deal with others, and the sorts of people you should be in business with. Neil always described the different types of people involved in ideation as builders or denters. Are you a builder, an eternal optimist who dreams big and has a high risk tolerance? Or are you a denter, someone skilled at seeing the problems, someone who pokes lots of holes and is reticent to take a risk? If you're starting a business alone and you're a builder, be sure you have a denter to balance you out, either in your company or as an adviser, and vice versa. Builders tend to get annoyed with denters. Denters are buzzkills, yes, but they also help you see what you otherwise may be blind to. And denters need builders, too.

You can't *just* be a naysayer; anyone can name problems all day long, but there comes a point when you have to reach a solution, and a builder can help do that. Neither is inherently good or bad: The best denters are able to problem solve or welcome new ideas. The best builders are willing to listen to denters, knowing they bring a 360-degree view.

At REBBL, we have a mix of builders and denters, and many people have both tendencies, although they may lean one way or the other. Palo is a builder. I was brought in as a cross between a builder and a denter. Jim, our consultant CFO, is a denter, but is really good at finding ways to make the build work—impressive for a CFO. (Unsurprisingly, CFOs and lawyers are almost always denters.) Palo, who is an artist by trade, "art directs" the taste and nutrition of our products at a pace that can be invigorating at times, and nerve-racking at others. As a builder, Palo is always convinced that he will find a way to solve any product problem so that it delivers on our extremely high standard for taste and nutrition. And he's almost always right! At one point Palo had been up for twenty-four hours straight, cramming on developing a product that was on a wicked-fast time line. Our director of sales, Mike, who has both builder and denter tendencies, told him bluntly, "This doesn't taste good at all." I was stunned at his directness, but Palo didn't flinch. I told the guys how impressed I was by how direct they were and how Palo, especially as an artist, was able to take it in stride. Palo said, "I've just learned to not react, to take it in, and to really understand why and what I need to do to fix it." That's an amazingly self-aware builder for you!

Understand whether you're a builder or a denter, so you know what and who you need to help you. Know what level of risk you need from a partner, and what level will make you crazy. Bring it all to the surface, where you can best see and assess.

Western Heroes and Lab Scientists

"I can't even envision being a billion-dollar company," said Rick Smith, a serial entrepreneur, "but I can envision what the achievements are I can shoot for in the next three months, and if I do it, it opens more doors. You never shoot for a home run . . . you can't control the home run. But it's easier than you think to get on first base. I want to be the company that can be on first base. Once you're safe, you can stand up and brush your jersey off and say, OK, where do I go? I've got options, I can take my time, I can survey the landscape, and if I get lucky and the landscape is right, I can score a run."

I love this advice, which stands in sharp contrast to "go big or go home," or, in the words of Ricky Bobby from *Talledega Nights*, "If you're not first, you're last." Those macho expressions have no place in the mind-set of an entrepreneur. Good entrepreneurs aren't John Wayne–esque heroes of old-time Westerns or farcical race car drivers. They're also not thrill seekers looking for that "one big climb." They're more like scientists, who hypothesize, test, and move forward. Or if you want to be a little more glamorous about it, they're like members of a well-practiced football team. Sure, when you're out on the field you're going to give it your all. But every bit of tedious practice, training, and drilling has put you in a position where the game—if not fully decided—is at least stacked in your favor. Players perpetually chip away at risk in order to win, and so do entrepreneurs.

A final word on risk, and it might be the most important: Listen to your gut. Call it intuition, mindfulness, or prayer, but when you have an uncomfortable feeling about something, listen to it. Don't go with the supplier who gives you the heebie-jeebies. Don't sign a contract when it feels like your pen is pulling you in the opposite direction. These are the times when it is Fear with a capital "F" speaking to you, and you want to listen to what she has to say. That doesn't mean walk away. But listen. Assess. And like the scientist, hypothesize, test, and move forward, one careful inch at a time.

CHAPTER 8

Self-Worth and Net Worth

The Entrepreneur and Money

From the landscape of Silicon Valley, a very clear picture emerges about the role of money. At the Stanford GSB, the sun shines, jazz plays from state-of-the-art (and yet uncannily tiny) speakers, a guy comes jogging through a sunny square, all toned, tanned muscles and expensive running gear. There's a good chance he's a millionaire. Many of the people visiting the GSB to teach or do a talk are *billionaires*. Many talk about changing the world. And many of the students, accustomed to being the best and the brightest, expect that they will be millionaires, too, and that they, too, will change the world. In hot startup cities like Boulder or Cambridge, the expectation is the same. Money might not literally be in the air, but it's evident in the buildings, the clothes, the cars, and the conversations, which often sound something like this: "Did your company make money? Sweet! You're a rock star!" or "Your company failed? Oh . . . sorry." There are now failure conferences and an effort to acknowledge failure, but it's still an uncomfortable conversation, and it never goes very deep. Money is still the measure. I worry about that individual who admits her company didn't make it, that bright, beautiful student who always defined herself as a "success" and has no clue how to handle failure without taking it very, and dangerously, personally. I worry about her a lot.

Now, look, I'm a businesswoman, and I'm not going to get all Kumbaya on you. You won't hear me say, "Forget money, it's only about love!" Money is the lifeblood of a company. It allows the company to thrive and add value in its customers' lives. Without money, what you've created cannot be in the world, plain and simple. But here's what's rarely discussed: money ain't everything, and we need to keep it in its place. If the journey is all about money and financial growth at all costs, it becomes hollow for everyone involved, and if the money doesn't come, the company dies and you lose the legacy you've created. If it's all you've been focused on, you feel like a failure. I've seen far too many wonderful people get sucked into thinking this way. They feel they *are* their company, and if that company's net worth plummets, so does their self-worth.

"Your brain develops based on where your attention is," said Dr. Christine Carter, a friend of mine who is also a coach, an author, a senior fellow at UC Berkeley's Greater Good Science Center, and an acclaimed sociologist. "If all your attention is focused on creating value in your company, conflating your company's external value with your own self-worth is an easy mistake to make. . . . This is not an individual mistake. This is a cultural mistake. Entrepreneurs are often raised and educated and even started their company in a culture that places a lot of value on the external, on how people look, how much they're worth—not intrinsic joys or what they personally find meaningful. If you've been taught to value extrinsic things—wins in school and on the athletic field, the things that an elite college or elite grad school values—you may not have asked yourself, 'Who am I and what do I want?'"

You don't have to look far to see our societal focus on external approval, or signs of it. We celebrate being acquired or our business reaching a high level of users by throwing flashy parties, and we share the word broadly, hoping the success will build on itself. We want to show others how well we've done, to say, "Look at me!" And when we lose, we face others turning away from us, saying, "I'm so sorry for your loss." I speak from personal experience. Patrick and I appreciated being supported through the aftermath of Blue Sky, but we could also see people look away with pity. And we proudly shared the news, walked a little taller, and looked people in the eye when we experienced the Plum sale. These public expressions of pride and shame are part of the way we live.

But we need to change the conversation. The very first step is to recognize it, to recognize the power of our money culture, to recognize that the equation we're so often writing is money=success, when it should be something much more nuanced. The equation should include impact, culture, love, and personal satisfaction. And that's just to begin with.

First, the Good News

Though there's much we need to do to change our "bottom line is king" mentality, from where I sit, it's already changing. When I was at Clif Bar, cofounder and owner Gary Erickson was really cognizant of holding the company accountable to multiple bottom lines—not just our profit. And he thought of profit as the way to make the ecosystem work, as opposed to the end goal. His five bottom lines were "sustaining our people, our community, our planet, our brand, and our business," and he held us accountable to delivering on all five. At that time, most consumers didn't know or care about the way the business ran—they just wanted their Clif Bar. Now things are different. Consumers are more informed, and they care *a lot* about where their food is coming from and how it's sourced. They are using their buying power to change the way companies do business—whether it's a food-related company or not. Pressure on the mega box store Walmart to improve the treatment of its workers, for instance, resulted in a pay increase (although it's still nowhere near what it should be). Consumer demand for organic food and strong ethics encouraged Target to initiate a "Made to Matter" program, in which it picks products from companies like Clif Bar, Plum, and Stonyfield Farms to feature in its stores. People don't want to work for companies without a heart, and consumers increasingly don't want to buy from them.

At the end of 2015, *Fast Company* compiled "20 Moments from the Past 20 Years That Moved the Whole World Forward," and the moment of 2012 was the rise of companies that do good.* Of note that year was the rise of the "B Corp," a certification for businesses that care about people, the planet, and profit. It's similar to what LEED is for environmental buildings. Companies can also be classified as a "benefit corporation," the designation when a company becomes legally bound to these principles. We are much more

---

* "20 Moments From the Past 20 Years That Moved the Whole World Forward," *Fast Company*, November 16, 2015.

used to C Corps, in which directors' only focus is to maximize profit for shareholders. In a B Corp, the company's duty to make money—while still important—is not paramount, and shareholders can even sue the directors for not carrying out the organization's social mission. The momentum toward B Corps is growing, and I wonder if we might see a day when there's a B Corp stock market or, better yet, when all companies are B Corps. A piece in *The New Yorker* explains, "In today's fiercely competitive business environment, one might assume that a company that thinks altruistically is doomed to failure. . . . Yet [B Corp-accredited] Warby Parker has had no trouble raising money from investors. . . . It's an important way for a company to attract and retain talented employees. Survey data show that workers—especially young ones—want to work for socially conscious companies and will take less compensation in exchange for a greater sense of purpose."[*]

Though not every state recognizes the B Corp, more are adopting it, including critical entrepreneur-friendly states like California and New York, and also states like Delaware, where many companies are incorporated. To apply to be a B Corp, you have to answer questions not only about the ingredients you use and if they are sustainably sourced (if you're a food company), but about how many of your employees telecommute, what their wages are, how much you as a company give back, and how you account for the impact of your offices on the environment. At Plum, we were B Corp-certified in our early days, and Neil convinced Campbell's, once it purchased Plum, to commit to keeping Plum a B Corp. Then they

---

[*]James Surowiecki, "Companies With Benefits," *The New Yorker*, August 4, 2014.

took it one step further and reincorporated the company as a public benefit corporation (PBC), the legal counterpart to the B Corp movement.

These are wonderful things to ask about, and they apply to any type of company—be it in tech or in the business of selling eyeglasses, like Warby Parker. But what's even more exciting to me is that the movement is changing the larger conversation, asking bigger questions about the role and responsibility of business. Do businesses always need to grow, especially at extremely fast clips? Is a business survivable without growth? Could a business plateau and stay there? Why do you always have to grow big? Can you have the growth be slower and give the money back to the community? Does business have a responsibility to lessen its footprint on the planet or, better yet, contribute to "climate drawdown"? Paul Hawken, an environmentalist, entrepreneur, and author who spearheads Project Drawdown, describes drawdown as "the point at which greenhouse gases in the atmosphere begin to decline on a year-to-year basis."* To me, this is not just about altruism, because without a protected planet, there will be no resources to do business with.

I'm far from the only person to have this opinion. The narrative is changing. A *New York Times Magazine* piece that listed the new "dream jobs" of millennials reported: "Survey after survey shows that millennials want to work for companies that place a premium on employee welfare, offer flexible scheduling, and, above all, bestow a sense of purpose."† Ac-

---

*Drawdown.org

†Jenna Wortham, "The New Dream Jobs," *New York Times Magazine*, February 28, 2016.

cording to a report by the World Economic Forum, 82 percent of millennials believe their generation can improve the world, and 84 percent believe it is their generation's duty to do so. Millennials want to support brands they trust to operate ethically. Seventy-one percent of millennials are looking for brands strong on the environment.° Given that millennials will make up 50 percent of the workforce by 2020, that's worth paying attention to. But it's not just millennials: 72 percent of all Americans think corporations should be doing more to address climate change.

Think how far we've come since my time at Clif Bar, over ten years ago. Every entrepreneur has to look forward, and in ten years, there simply will be less room for companies that don't think about metrics other than the financial ones.

The Other Good News: Multiple Bottom Lines Are Good for You, Too

When you are less focused on a singular, fiduciary bottom line, it's naturally easier to have a healthier, more multidimensional relationship with your life's work. If your profits fall short for a quarter, you can find ease of knowing that you improved lives in that same quarter, or that you helped the environment.

Perhaps no one knows this quite so well as Jeffrey Hollander. He's famous for cofounding Seventh Generation, a brand of environmentally responsible products. From diapers

° "Engaging Tomorrow's Consumer," report by the World Economic Forum's Sustainable Consumption initiative, prepared in collaboration with Accenture, January 2013, http://www3.weforum.org/docs/WEF_RC_EngagingTomorrows Consumer_Report_2013.pdf.

to detergent, Seventh Generation is committed to being transparent about its products' ingredients and being sensitive to the environment. But for a long time it struggled financially. "My self-worth," said Jeffrey, "was for most of my life connected in a very unhealthy way to the success of the business. . . . The success of the business was most of my own identity, and it was very hard to feel good about myself if the business wasn't doing well. I still struggle today with trying to redefine success in a way that is not tied to sales and profits." Note, reader, that he still struggles. I'm not saying this transition is easy!

Now, along with his daughter, Jeffrey runs Sustain, a company that sources and sells sustainable, fair trade condoms and other sexual-wellness products. According to its marketing materials, Sustain's goal is to "educate and help people connect the dots between condoms and hunger, health care, poverty, and climate change."

Jeffrey said, "The struggle is to continually remind myself that we can be very successful as a business in spite of the fact that we might not be generating the growth and profits we'd like to, because if we think about the business in a more holistic sense, everything we do has positive impacts. And we need to learn to value those positive impacts that are outside the most traditional metrics." If there's a moment when Sustain's not hitting its numbers, he said, they're still in the positive from an educational perspective, or in the positive from the changes they're making to repair a broken supply chain. There's a lot to feel good about at the end of the day, he said, even if from the data perspective it's been a difficult one.

Jeffrey has learned—and is still learning—not to get caught up in measuring everything all the time, but to instead rest comfortably, knowing that his work is in keeping with his values. Now imagine how hard this separation would be for someone who isn't looking at the bigger-picture impact of his or her company. "I don't have much interest in businesses that don't have a social purpose," Jeffrey said. "I have little interest in people who are struggling with the challenges of self-worth/ net worth in a traditional context, because you've chosen having a path where you'll live or die by those business metrics."

Although I personally celebrate everything Jeffrey expressed, I don't want to speak only to the choir. I'm writing this book in part to help all aspiring and current entrepreneurs be able to see that there is more to business than the traditional metrics. That having this bigger picture can lead to better company performance because the company's whole network—including customers, employees, investors, suppliers, and partners—is proudly working toward a purpose that makes a difference. Having this bigger picture helps you feel good about what you're doing beyond the ups and downs of business. It keeps your life aligned with your values, and helps you course-correct when you feel out of line. Having a greater purpose with your business reminds you that you're a valuable person in spite of numbers.

At REBBL, Palo (who happens to be the son of Project Drawdown leader Paul Hawken) and I look at the bigger picture constantly. Palo is a lovely, grounded person whose primary goal is to bring the gift of something better into the world, and he believes REBBL is that something better. We want the company to be financially successful, to be viable and sustainable, because that will mean we will get the product we're passionate about into the hands of people whom it will help. And if REBBL sales increase, we can positively affect the growers of our ingredients and support our nonprofit partner's efforts to eradicate human trafficking. If the money comes, great—but the money is secondary; it's a means to an end.

For a company to work in the long run, it has to find a sustainable, long-term, profitable business model. Sometimes that takes time; REBBL took from 2011 to 2014 to find the right business model. First we had to hit on the right product. Our tonics were doing well, but elixirs were off the charts. The market told us that elixirs were the horse to ride, and we did so by investing in elixirs and discontinuing tonics. Although this example focused on our growth rate, there are choices we make every day at REBBL that seem to act against the traditional profit bottom line. We want the people who grow our ingredients to earn a living wage, so we choose to be fair trade, which is more expensive. So are organic ingredients. These are all investment choices based on why we are in business. One of our seven employees, Dani, will become dedicated to measuring and amplifying our impact, which means we're investing more in our mission at a time when we could use all hands on deck just to drive profit. To us, it's the human and the planetary impact that is just as important as the impact on growth and profits. There are countless choices like this and many tension points, but there is beauty in that tension. It's in that tension that you find the creative solutions that ultimately may lead to greater growth and profits.

Working within this tension inspires innovation and leads to viable, valuable businesses. Consider the example of Not for Sale. The nonprofit was working to find a solution to slave labor in modern-day Peru. That led to the idea to start a sustainable for-profit company that uses a native Peruvian herb, cat's claw, in a beverage. This is REBBL's origin story. Or consider Seventh Generation. In its early days, the company's cleaning solutions were environmentally safe, yet sometimes challenging to use to get deep cleaning. Seventh Generation used that tension as a source of inspiration, and it led to the development of effective and still mission-driven new products. Similar innovations have been the result of a growing consumer trend to cut down on eating meat for health and environmental reasons. Vegetarian food tastes better than ever before, thanks to the innovations of companies like Gardein, which makes plant protein–based meals. In 1993, Google cofounder Larry Page conceived of a driverless transportation system in response to a challenge to break down the barriers to peoples' ability to fulfill their potential. Google is still working on that system today.

Whether you consider yourself a do-gooder or not, challenge yourself to tap into the values that are important to you, and ask how your business can reflect those. Is it by supporting a Little League team? The library? Local food banks? What is the greater purpose in your work beyond just a monetary one?

Now that I've said my piece, it's your turn. Take this prompt: "The purpose of my company is . . ." Try to fill it in with three things that have nothing to do with money. Can you do it? Do you not want to? What would your employees say? Also, ask yourself what happens if your company fails financially. Will you be okay with yourself? Will there be something to celebrate?

The Epic Adventure

Adjusting your end goal to be more multifaceted is important, but it's not enough. You can still get so consumed by your business that it becomes your identity. Remember what Christine

Carter said: "Your brain develops based on where your attention is." So move some of that attention around.

Start from a place where you say, "I'm going on an adventure. I don't know what's going to happen. I might come out with a huge amount of money; I might come out with nothing. But I am going to protect myself from being made or broken by the financial gain or loss of it. I'm going to prepare well, embrace this adventure, learn something, savor the experience of a lifetime, all while cheering myself and my team because we have the courage to do it."

That's the feeling I had when I entered a mountain bike race in Lake Tahoe with several other women from Clif Bar. It was a team race in which you take turns riding laps for twenty-four straight hours on a mountain. The course was crazy, with ruts, bumps, huge climbs, and sheer drop-offs. I went over my handlebars and had an intense migraine, but got back on the bike to do my lap. My teammate Kory got a piece of wood lodged in her leg and two beestings. She went to the emergency room to get stitches, but got back on the bike to do her next lap. Rochelle broke her crank, went back to get it fixed, then finished her lap. On her night lap, she saw a bear. Mari's chain broke in the middle of her lap, but she continued on foot for the sake of the team. Elizabeth was the only one who survived without an incident, but she was completely wiped out at the end. Yet I'll remember that experience forever. It wasn't about winning—that wasn't even close to a possibility. It wasn't pretty. We were slow, but it felt like a huge accomplishment to all of us. It was the experience, the adventure of doing it, that mattered.

I advise Rip Pruisken and Marco de Leon, the founders of Rip van Wafels, who are a fantastic embodiment of this mentality in business. Rip and Marco are so immersed in and excited about what they're doing. Their company is their passion, and they see business as a powerful vehicle to live their purpose—to have a positive impact. They don't view growth, sales, and valuation targets as the main goal but rather a yardstick to gauge how well they're living their purpose through their business. They see maintaining control of their business as an important driver; it's what will enable them to help the company have a greater impact—as they define it—in the long run. They're taking it slow and are not accepting a lot of outside capital, but are totally eager to learn everything they can about running a company.

It's joyful to talk to them. It's not that their every day is sunshine and roses; in fact, some days totally suck, but on balance, they take great pride and joy in what they do each day. Rip said he thinks what helps him keep a handle on everything is that he always revisits his motives. And he doesn't just revisit them, he questions them like a professor using the Socratic method. "You need to ask, 'Why am I doing this? Why is it important to me?' And then question your answer," he said.

"Let's say you're doing this because you want to be financially free one day," said Rip of the process he uses to question himself. "You'd think, 'Okay, well, why is that important?' and then you answer that. You have to ask, 'What does "financially free" mean?' and then you define *that*. And then you say, 'Why have I defined it to be what it is?'. . . . The process of questioning, and in parallel, meditation, has given me clarity. . . . It's that constant questioning and evolution in our own consciousness that makes me look at the world in a different way and gives me a deeper sense of purpose." In other words, Rip isn't looking at the bottom line in any sort of rote way. Rip and Marco are constantly questioning what it means to the grand adventure of their lives.

It's the same idea behind Mark Rampolla's frequent dialogue with his wife, Maura, or behind Patrick's meaningful looks at me when I'm going overboard. I might think I *need* to send just those last three emails, or to clear through my inbox, or that if I quit giving direction for two minutes, then everything will stop. I might be so busy reacting that I don't stop to listen, or to really think. I might be so blinded by my need to keep up momentum that I completely lose the big picture. It's when I do this, when any of us do this, that we get hyperfocused and are most at risk of spinning in anxious circles.

There's a lot I've learned about stopping the spinning and savoring the experience. I not only focus on the business conversation with my teammates, but I pay attention to how smart and thoughtful they are and how much I'm enjoying an intellectual and philosophical conversation. I make sure that I'm able to spend the time with them not only that I need to, but also the time when I simply just *want* to. Mike and Jim make me laugh, and I love mentoring Dani and Rachel, women who are in the first phase of their careers. It's a pleasure to listen to Palo pontificate, when we actually have time just to talk. We send each other texts during the weekend, sharing the fun we're having outside work, to keep ourselves accountable for *having* fun. I constantly reflect on these positive moments with my team. Each day, I try to think about an interaction that made me really happy. Then on Fridays, I try to reflect on the fun times I had in my week. This doesn't mean I ignore the hard parts, but I'm shining a light on the good parts and reminding myself, "Sheryl, relax—this is *fun.*"

It's a way to make sure you're not white-knuckling your way through on the way to a goal that you may never achieve. Because if worse comes to worst, you don't want to look back and say, "Well, that sucked—I just wasted three years of my life." You want to instead say—and mean—"What an awesome, totally wild ride!"

Assess the Value of Money in Your Life

When Patrick and I were dealing with the fallout from Blue Sky, it took no time for us to agree that we needed to sell our home. While of course I wish we hadn't gotten so far in over our heads financially, and I don't exactly look back on the many moves and different addresses we had afterward with fondness, I'm proud that we were able to see what needed to be done, and that we were able to reset.

We have seen friends and neighbors in California who cannot let go of their home because of its outsize meaning in their lives, the way it conveys status to them. I get it. There were definitely times when I felt, *I worked so hard to get to where I was . . . and look where I am now.* But Patrick and I didn't waffle for a moment about whether to give up the house or not. We knew we could sit and obsess, thinking about how embarrassing it was that we had to move, or that our friends would see our new place. Instead we rolled up our sleeves and recognized it was just a house. We could see that it was all relative, and that ours was a high-class problem. We had to watch every penny we spent, there were some nights that I just broke down and cried because of how much we'd lost, but we were on balance doing okay. We constantly told ourselves that this was our new reality. We can't live in the past; we need to move forward from where we stand.

Money can easily distort good sense. More money must equal a better life, we think. But that's not so. There comes a point of diminishing returns. When it comes to money and parenting, for instance, Malcolm Gladwell points out that it looks more like an inverted U curve: the more money you have, the *harder* it is to parent.˙ Similarly, I think that once you get in the mind-set of "I always have to make more to be better," your happiness goes way down.

To keep a healthy self-worth/net worth separation, you have to continually ask yourself what role money is serving in your endeavor. Is money itself becoming your identity? What role do status symbols play in your life? What are the other things that you're proud of? What do other people on your team express that they're proud of? What is your family proud of? We always ask our kids what they are grateful for, and we share our gratitude. We all invariably say "a loving, close family." This dialogue always grounds me on the hard days that test our family values. These may seem like silly questions, but we don't ask them often enough, and we then find ourselves following the money path. It's easy to do, because money is so easily measurable, so black and white (or, er, green). The other stuff requires us to think deeper and get in touch with who we really are. And by doing so, we may experience the demons of what we are not. Exploring our self-worth is hard work, but it also happens to be how we get to know ourselves and discover what's really important to us.

˙Malcolm Gladwell, *David and Goliath: Underdogs, Misfits, and the Art of Battling Giants* (New York: Little, Brown, 2013), 50.

The Great Challenge of Investors

It would be irresponsible for me to write a chapter about net worth and self-worth without discussing what so often is a party to conflating the two: investors. You may have a good head on your shoulders. You may want to do good in the world, have a great, fun company, set boundaries, and savor each day. But investors can still bring you down. Or perhaps your investors are great, supportive, and helpful all the way. Good for you! The thing is, it's incredibly hard to determine what an investor will be like when you first meet him or her, and it's virtually impossible to avoid dealing with assholes altogether. I've had investors who have felt entitled to call me at all hours, and investors who have freely doled out insults. Once when I was giving a presentation to my board, I had an investor text me—midpresentation, mind you—to tell me everything I was doing wrong in it. That shook my confidence, and instead of managing a good, robust dialogue in the meeting, I became focused on "I'm such a fuckup." Talk about a threat to self-worth! On balance, investors still value the traditional metrics more than anything. And fair enough—your company is a financial investment to them, and they want a return on that investment. But they can have very different approaches in how they help or hurt you get there.

Investors can also be incredibly supportive, and I've had my share of those individuals, too. With the good ones, their central question is "How can I help you?" When waters get a little rough, they're a calming force that helps you get through it by offering sound counsel. Investors can also offer new opportunities through great contacts, ideas they've seen that work, and insight about issues that you may have never experienced but that they've successfully navigated. *But,* if you're worried about your tendency to focus obsessively on the bottom line, and if you think you'll have a hard time setting boundaries, think twice about bringing on an investor. You do have options.

For one, you can try to bootstrap it yourself. With many businesses now, especially Internet-based ones, you can start a business on the cheap. This allows you to have some runway space to test what works in the business, to improve the selling points and valuation of your company, before you take on an investor, if you even need to. Even consumer product companies can be started on a small scale to test a concept if you have some capital to get you through.

You can also bring in family or angel investors who, if you set up the relationship right, will let you run your business as you see fit. The challenge with family, of course, is that you risk losing their money, and that can be hard to deal with every Thanksgiving. Angel investors can work well, but you can also end up with a long list of angels that gets harder and harder to manage over time. And the majority of them don't tend to provide resources beyond money. There are also more and more socially responsible investors every day, and even values-based investment banking organizations.

If you decide to take on institutional investors such as venture capitalists, as I've done, a few words of advice:

- Think carefully about who that investor is. Ask all investors about what they consider to be their successes and failures and why. Remember, you are interviewing them as much as, if not more than, they are interviewing you. What is their past experience? Why did they change jobs? Spend a lot of time talking face-to-face in a nonbusiness setting. Discuss hypothetical scenarios. Is this investor someone who really gets what your mission is? Is she someone who will respect your boundaries? Is she someone who will try to oust you at the first sign of financial struggle, even if the other bottom lines are performing well? Will she stand up to another board member who's out of line? How will she handle the hard times? What has she done in her past? Are there any stories floating around the Internet about her? Don't just rely on the potential investor's word. What do other entrepreneurs or investment firms that have worked with her think? Some people won't share, so keep asking others. Check references you're given and others that you're not (that's what VCs will do about you, by the way). What does your gut say?

- Don't be desperate. It's very dangerous to get to a point where you'll take any dollar you can get. Finding the right investor match takes time, and it is so, so important. Fundraising is hard. You get a lot of doors that open for a fleeting moment (investors are usually willing to talk with entrepreneurs, especially if you find a way to get an introduction to them), but they can close very quickly. You usually find that they're closed only because the investor no longer responds to your emails or takes your calls.

- Set realistic expectations for growth with your investors, and devise ways to meet those expectations that are humane, ethical, and in line with your company's mission. I learned that the hard way when my first forecast for Plum was way too optimistic. You want to have a good balance of optimism and realism. It's really hard to try to set up these parameters when you just need money desperately.

- Appreciate the tension. Investors often ask difficult, challenging questions. This is a great thing that will make you stronger. Have the humility to really listen, and yet have the confidence to push back when something doesn't feel right. An investor I really like once said, "I will push entrepreneurs, but if they tell me they feel strongly, I support them every time and I won't go back on my word to support them." That's a great investor.

- Be careful how much of your company you give investors. (And make sure you have a really good lawyer to represent your interests.) If you talk to investors who don't seem to get how important it is for you to have a big stake, deeply question yourself as to whether or not it's a good fit.

- Learn the "clearing" model of communication. One entrepreneur, Bart, explained how he's used it several times with a difficult investor to great effect. "The idea of clearing is that you get it on the table," he said. "You say 'I value this relationship, we are important partners, and I want to clear this.'" Then you go through the story, your accounting of how it made you feel when something happened. Then the other person reflects back to you what he or she heard you say. It forces honest communication, and the whole point is that you're not going to solve the problem. But you walk away knowing you've been heard and the person squarely knows where you stand. "It's put me in a place where it's clear that I'm going to call it anytime I see a discrepancy, anytime I see something that is contrary to a productive and aligned discussion," Bart said. "I'm going to call it, and I'm going to call it hard. What that's done is to create a manage-up environment—I'm not very easy to pull something over at this point."

For my part, I've made some poor choices in investors. At times, I jumped too fast to get the money, only to come to regret it later. Other times, I've had investors who have offered wonderful support and mentorship. At REBBL, we have investors who were also entrepreneurs themselves. They're able to see things through very different eyes, and to help me at the right times and in the right ways with introductions and advice. When I wanted to bring in some agencies to help us build our PR, social media, and branding capabilities, one of my investors gave me contacts for the best of the best in the beverage business. Given his relationship with them (he's like a pied piper for the natural food and beverage world), they dropped everything to work with us.

Several of my investors deeply relate to what I'm going through, and I feel their support every step of the way. It's made the ride exciting and fun. It feels like we're all in it together, versus me standing on one end, alone with a flimsy shield; and the investors on the other side with their scorecard and a whip.

The Grand Scale of Perspective

As a founder or CEO, you don't get a lot of validation. You're often cheering others on, but it's not really anyone's job to cheer you on. (Although it should be the job of investors and boards. Inspiration, motivation, and optimism help create great leaders and companies.) And it's likely that you got to where you are because you've always reached for those signs of validation. When they don't come anymore, it's incredibly tempting to peek at that P&L again and again and to say, "See! There it is! I *am* doing a good job!" But to be a healthy entrepreneur, you have to have validation that comes from yourself instead. You have to have the strength to be able to say, "I killed it," when you know you have. Or if things aren't going well, you have to have the strength to say, "I'm having a rough time, but I know my values are in line, and so I'm going to show myself some compassion."

I talked with a woman named Jane recently who has a great and thriving company, one that came from her heart as a mom. She has another idea she wants to see in the world, but she's afraid to try it out because of the pressure she thinks she'll feel to be traditionally "successful" twice. She's focused on that external validation, and she hates it. She's trying to have the courage to start the business and feels every day a bit closer to taking the first step. It's possible that the best thing that could happen to her is to experience a failure. Entrepreneurs are so often fast movers, going from one thing to another at lightning speed, spinning so much that we can't be with ourselves to think. But a failure can force you to sit back and ground yourself, to feel what you're feeling, to explore those feelings with a friend, your significant other, or a therapist so that you can find a place of peace. Everything we've talked about in this chapter—setting multiple bottom lines, savoring the adventure, examining your relationship with money, and protecting yourself from overzealous investors— will help shift validation from the external to the internal. External measurements are only growing in influence, which increases the importance of having a strong internal compass. The "Quantified Self" movement, in which we measure everything from our steps to our sleep, is growing in popularity. We can be so obsessed with numbers that we forget to live.

Numbers are a point of context that can give us direction in our lives, but they are not our lives.

I know a little something about obsession with numbers. I want to leave you here with a thought about another meter that was of significant importance to me: a bathroom scale. A scale can be a great tool; it's a way of keeping track of your health. But in an incorrect mind, like mine was, it starts to take on a different meaning. The *number* it reflects starts to take on a different meaning. If that number's not going down, you feel that you're a failure. But when your mind is healthy, you can stand on that scale and let the number simply be information. It's not bad or good, it just is. It doesn't equal your worth.

Put your business in perspective. Are you healthy enough to step on that scale? Is the number it shows simply *information*? Or is it a *judgment*? If the latter, if that number is more important to you than anything else, then please hear me: it's time to step away before you get sick.

CHAPTER 9

Modestly Naked

The Entrepreneur and Bold Humility

During a pretty intense period at Plum, the management team told me they were frustrated. But I didn't hear that *I* was the one they were frustrated with. We needed to get our operations in order, our sales in order, and our systems in order. I was under a lot of pressure from the board to make those things happen. But Plum was all about innovation, and I was acutely aware that Neil and others were concerned that innovation be at the top of the priority list. I didn't want to let anyone down, and I thought that, as a team, we could manage it all—that we could make it work somehow, by sheer force of will.

I was terrified of making the wrong call and failing, and so went full speed ahead on everything, when really I should have set clearer priorities. When the team complained that they were too busy and working too many late hours, I justified it by saying entrepreneurial environments are crazy. That it would get better when we could bring on more people. That work at that pace was needed to push through, even though we had no time to rest and recover. Also, in an effort to make everyone feel included and heard, I'd involve too many people in too many discussions and then wait too long to make a decision, wanting to make sure we addressed everyone's concerns. What killed me about this whole thing was that it went on for far too long without my realizing it was *me* who was frustrating people. I thought I was open enough that my team would tell me if I wasn't giving them something they needed. They were—in their actions and their cry for help—but I just wasn't hearing it until they all came to me at once. Why hadn't I seen it coming?

C. S. Lewis wrote, "Failures are finger posts on the road to achievement." Or, as I usually say, "Innovation is born from the shit that goes wrong." The takeaway from either phrasing is the same: failures are really what build us as people. They give us empathy and make us wise. From the psychological to the business sectors, the benefits of admitting to and learning from failures are well documented. But you wouldn't know this to look at the self-congratulation-fest that is entrepreneurship.

Some of this harkens back to what we covered in chapter 3. Entrepreneurs spend their days trying to inspire people to follow them—to buy into their vision either by working for them, buying their product, or investing money in their company. When you are in sales mode, or fundraising mode, your role is to defuse doubt. Your line is: "This product is better than anything you've ever seen, this company is great, and you should feel nothing but confident that I can lead it to become a very valuable business!" But as Jeffrey Hollander said, "Entrepreneurs confuse the process of needing to sell to a customer or investor with what honest conversation and dialogue is about."

I first heard the phrase "bold humility" from Frances Moore Lappé, the author of the revolutionary book *Diet for a Small Planet*. What those two simple words used together says to me is that we have to balance the yin and the yang, the traditionally "male" quality of being bold with the traditionally "female" quality of having humility. A visionary leader who always knows the next step but never acknowledges fear or fault has work to do. He is missing out on a fuller, and better, leadership experience. So is the person who is so humble that she has a hard time believing she does have the right answers, and that she does know how to chart a way forward. The yin and the yang have a lot to teach one another.

Blind Spots: Be Honest with Yourself about Your Shortcomings

We all have shortcomings, we all have flaws, and yet we employ different layers of protection to hide them from ourselves. They're our blind spots, and we aim to keep them that way. Chances are good you've seen someone else's blind spot. They often appear when people are so sure of themselves. Take, for instance, the founder who genuinely feels she's a great manager—she prides herself on it, even—but she doesn't seem to recognize that she's only ever managed three people, and two of them have quit.

There are multiple factors at play with entrepreneurial blind spots, and one of them is that we can't forgive ourselves for not being right. We have such high ideals and attach so much judgment to reaching them. We have to be the perfect parent, the perfect community citizen, the perfect spouse, perfectly in control. While it's challenging to admit your wrongs to others, it can feel *impossible* to admit them to yourself. We believe anything short of perfection will result in letting other people, and ourselves, down.

We suffer for it, because it's an impossible standard. And our business suffers, too. Sought-after board member Brad Barnhorn, who founded the Fantasia Fresh Juice brand that he merged into Naked Juice, thinks blind perfectionism is a particularly dangerous dragon that entrepreneurs must slay. "Unfortunately, many entrepreneurs came to the conclusion early in life through family and social dynamics that the way the world works is that perfection without exception is the price of admission to be loved, respected, and accepted," he said. "It's a very scarcity-based view of the world that ultimately creates frustration and disconnection within oneself and the business even when things may in fact be going incredibly well."

The mind-set of perfectionism and scarcity is one as a board member that he tries to help entrepreneurs see and change.

I know people who are fantastic at growing a company from the $100 million level to the $200 million or even billion-dollar level. They are not so good at scaling a startup. Likewise, there are folks who are great at the startup and early-growth levels, but who struggle leading a company at the $20 million-plus range, when processes and systems are desperately needed. I know based on all my experiences that my favorite parts of the journey are when a company has about $2 to $50 million in revenue, when it's starting to get traction. The team still feels like a family and the company is beginning to have an impact. I'm aware now that I don't love the stage when an organization becomes focused largely on process, and I don't have a strong desire to start another company from scratch. I'm okay with that now, but for a long time I believed I needed to love it all, to do it all, and to do it all perfectly. I'm also aware that I have blind spots even in the range I love, so I fill in those gaps with great people. For example, I don't have the patience for the details of creating spreadsheets and building financial models myself. That's not where I'm strong. But I love the stories that numbers tell. Given that, I always need a great finance partner at my side. Entrepreneurs often don't admit such inclinations to themselves because they *want* to be good at everything. They think they *should* be good at everything. It's simply not okay with them not to be all things to all people. But if they could see and accept where they are good and where they aren't so good, they'd have a much bigger world open to them. At the most logical level, they would then know that they needed to hire someone to fill in their weak spots, and they would know just what qualities they were looking for from that person.

Sometimes our blind spot has nothing to do with perfectionism, as it rather lives within an area of our identity where we're typically strong, and that's precisely why we don't see it. I am solidly in this camp. I have always prided myself on being open and accessible, and willing to listen to and take feedback. I aim to be a leader who is supportive and a good collaborator. I don't consider myself an autocratic leader, and I respect other people's point of view. I feel strongly about helping people to feel empowered. I am constantly asking for feedback. That's my strength, but it has also been my blind spot, as it was when I was trying to make everyone feel included at Plum, when what they really needed was a strong leader to set priorities.

I've gotten much better at this, but I'm still very cognizant of it as a potential blind spot. I talk to one of REBBL's board members each week. I asked him to reflect on my leadership in regards to making decisions. He said, "I have noticed that you're great about asking for input from the team and from board members. You're surrounded by really talented people, so I understand why you're doing that." But he also told me that I have a lot more latitude to simply inform people what I'm doing and move forward, versus always inviting input. "Trust your instincts and get points of view when you really need them. You have so much latitude before you become overly aggressive, and your board will tell you if you're getting anywhere close." What a great reminder that I still have work to do on my blind spot. I can be bold without fearing I'm crossing a line—I'm likely not even close to the line.

The best way to illuminate these blind spots is to walk straight into them. Ask yourself what you most pride yourself on, what you think your strongest characteristics are. Then check them—with yourself, with those close to you personally, and with those you work with. Of course, be sure that people are free to give feedback honestly and with impunity. Don't just use the catch-all phrase "You can come to me with everything!" Instead, ask more probing questions. Say, "I consider myself a [insert adjective here] person, and I'm proud to be. But I also think this pride means I'm not seeing things as they are. You have clearer vision than I do on this subject— what do you think? Are there ways I could be better at this?"

There's one other cause of blind spots, and that's an inflated ego. Remember the story of Icarus from Greek mythology? His father made him wings of wax so he could fly, but warned him not to fly too close to the sun or the wings would melt. Icarus got carried away, flew too close to the sun, and bye-bye, Icarus. So, clearly, hubris like this has been around since Zeus. When you are an entrepreneur, and particularly if you are a financially successful entrepreneur, you have many people who want to stand in your light. Everyone looks to you for answers. You start to get talked about in the press. They will tell you that you are brilliant, that you can do no wrong. We see this all the time in the realm of sports (Tiger Woods), entertainment (Bill Cosby), and politics (I can think of a political scandal or a thousand that were created by mini-Icaruses, but to keep it simple: Donald Trump).

Ego-driven blind spots are much more common than you might think, even in companies that are small. Simply put, owning a company can go to your head. Financial success can go to your head. You are proud of your company, as you should be, and believe everyone wants to be a part of it and, therefore, associated with you. And maybe they do. And because people want to be a part of it, it's easy to then think you are infallible. Also, everyone wants to emulate what you do, so they seek out any information about you through the press, trying to get a meeting with you, anything to touch you and have your magic rub off on them.

A small company that sells mountain bikes has been very successful for years. They have a great culture they're proud of. They have fun together, and they relish their antiestablishment flair. If small business was a high school, they'd be the cool kids. But what they didn't see for a while was the way they were alienating those who worked for them. Their general line—"We are so awesome that people are lining up to work here"—meant that they didn't take their employees' complaints very seriously. And many more employees felt they couldn't complain at all. The moral here is as simple as the Greek myth: don't get so full of yourself that you fail to see your wings are melting.

Fail Publicly: Be Honest with Others about Your Shortcomings

In my early days at Clif when I was running the company's marketing, I was always the cheerleader. I truly thought everything was fantastic, but I also saw it as my responsibility to make sure everyone felt excited all the time. We were growing really fast, from a shoot-from-the-hip type of place to something much bigger. Emotions were high, and people were thinking, "The company's changing—what's going to happen? Are we still the same company we once were?" People were nervous, and when they expressed it to me, I always said, "Don't worry! It'll be great!" Carole, a bright member of my team whom I respected and who was highly influential with her peers, finally said, point-blank, "Sheryl, people won't be able to trust you if you don't show them that you get that this is a hard transition." It was a huge moment for me. I realized that I hadn't acknowledged people and their humanity. How could we move forward with the growth of this company and not talk about our worries or acknowledge one another's fears? I was invalidating their worries by denying that I had any. I hadn't done it out of meanness, obviously. It was well intentioned, and people knew that. But it was also wrong. I knew what I had to do. I pulled the team together around our big round table and said, "I'm sorry. I've been so busy cheerleading, I lost sight of how hard this transition is for many of us, including me. I'm confident that we'll get through it but I'm feeling pain along the way. I know you are, too, as you've tried to express it but I haven't fully heard you. Let's talk about it." That opened a wonderful, real, and very human conversation. Not only that, it brought us closer and made us more trusting as a team.

Christine Carter said, "There is enormous power in exposing yourself emotionally, because it allows people to hear you from an openhearted place that enables you to be successful." I couldn't agree more, and I firmly believe that when you show vulnerability, as I eventually did at Clif, people are *more* attracted to you as a leader, not less.

I needed to model humility and be honest about my fears so that others would feel they could be honest with me about theirs. What if someone was completely in over his head? What if someone was struggling so much that he was about to drop a pretty huge ball? Admitting you're struggling doesn't mean you're weak. In fact, it means you're doing a great job, because you're so self-aware that there's no way you're going to let things fall apart on your watch. (Of course, if you're always struggling, then perhaps you're in the wrong position, and it's time for a humble conversation to get you in the right place.) As a leader, it's important to have a culture in which people can come to you with information and get help before it's too late. This is especially important in a startup, where everyone is doing everything and there are few people, if any, to turn to for help when things get hard. Maybe someone has a little extra bandwidth and can help you out if you're swamped, even if it's just for a day. Or perhaps a supportive board member or adviser can jump in, roll up her sleeves, and help. Or perhaps someone can help you reprioritize so the right things get done when they need to.

Before I started at REBBL, Palo was crazy busy. He was doing the CEO job, managing a board that was bigger than the number of employees, running production, creating new products, and starting to fundraise. Dani, one of his first employees, would notice his angst and step in to help him get it done. Palo didn't even need to ask. Dani would say, "You need help—let me help you." Palo was humble enough to say, "You're right. I need help. Help me." What an outstanding model for leadership.

Owning such moments of being overwhelmed is key, as is owning missteps. Being open about failure can be a huge benefit to a culture, as I've learned time and again. When I was working on Luna, the low-carb craze of the early 2000s caused us to lose over $20 million in sales in one year. Retailers threatened that we would lose a lot of shelf space if we didn't come out with a low-carb bar. We finally relented and made one, as natural and tasty as possible, but due to the inherent challenges in low carb, it wasn't up to our standards. It was called Luna Glow. You have probably never heard of it, because it crashed and burned in six months.

But here's what I learned from that experience: I had a chance to influence the culture, to learn from my mistake, and to promote experimentation and an openness to fail. So I shouted from the rooftops that I had screwed up and had made a bad judgment call. Rather than burying the failure and explaining it away, saying it was due to the waning of the low-carb craze or that it was another team member's fault, I took full accountability for it and was transparent about it with our team. I explained that it was my fault—I'd made the call to go for it. I told the team that I wanted their help to figure out the lessons from the experience. This openness gave others permission to do the same and cleared the way for free-flowing, productive collaboration. I explained that Luna Glow taught me to stay true to our brand. It didn't mean we shouldn't adapt to the market, but that we must always adapt in a way that maintained the essence of our brand— our authenticity. This experience forced us to become deeply grounded in who we were as a brand. It helped us to re-embrace what we stood for as a company, and we drove an enormous amount of innovation thereafter.

"I have a talk I occasionally give about my ten biggest mistakes, and I think people learn more from that than from the ten smartest things I've done," said Jeffrey Hollander. Sharing our mistakes, he said, "keeps us humble and it keeps us real. The worst thing you can do is hide those mistakes, because then they never get fixed. You also model that for your employees, creating an environment where it's not safe to make mistakes. And by having an all-confident exterior, you create less space for other people to rise to challenges and offer the best idea there is to move forward."

Admitting mistakes is one important step on the way to entrepreneurial humility; apologizing is another. Saying "I'm sorry" makes people feel heard and validated, even if you're not sure if it's your fault or not. Sometimes it just doesn't matter. Yet for many reasons, we don't use that powerful phrase. You don't have to fall on the sword like a martyr— you can still hold other people accountable. However, if the accountability is unclear and an error is getting in the way of moving forward, just say "I'm sorry that this happened. Let's fix it and figure out how we can avoid this kind of situation in the future." Especially if you're a CEO, you're the one ultimately to blame when responsibility isn't clear, so it's important to take ownership, fix it, and then hold others accountable for their role.

Just the other day, I was working through a budget issue with Palo and our CFO, Jim. A number in the budget didn't match what we remembered it to be. We couldn't figure out why the change had happened. I vaguely remembered a conversation with Palo in which we had agreed to a lower number, but none of us could remember the details. Admittedly, I had a moment of "Someone else caused this. Someone else didn't make sure the numbers were reconciled." But then I took a step back and said, "Look, guys, I'm the ultimate P&L holder, and I didn't realize it wasn't reconciled. That's my accountability, and I'm sorry. Let's get the number right and change the process. From now on, whenever a number changes, we'll notate it in the notes section and describe why it happened. And let's always make sure the three of us have done so, and check the updated version." We all moved on and got back to business a little better than before. "Sorry" can go a long way.

Henry was a serious, hardworking cook who worked for a small catering business that had a lot of trouble finding its footing. The founders offered the brass ring of partial ownership to him, and then pulled the offer back as the company grew quickly and the structure changed. In the course of things, it was probably the right business move, but there's no question it left some messy baggage in its wake. Henry expressed his frustration with the many changes and how lousy it felt from his side. The founders explained their reasoning for the decision and asked Henry what would make him feel better going forward. This was all good and productive, except the founders didn't say the two words that Henry needed to hear: We're sorry. It wouldn't have undone the harm, and they still needed to focus on making things right with Henry from a financial point of view. But those two words could have validated Henry's feelings of injury. They could have said, "Hey, you know what? We can totally see how this sucks for you. You thought you were going to be an owner, and then things changed. That would be a really crappy feeling. We're really sorry that we didn't handle things better from the beginning. It makes us sad to have caused you any pain."

What did the founders have to lose by apologizing in this situation? They weren't worried that Henry would sue them. Were they worried Henry would lord it over them forever if they admitted their fault? Perhaps. But their mistake was so clear to them and to Henry anyway, why not just name it as such? Pride, fear, and ego all play into this, but most of all, I think that they felt it wouldn't show leadership if they said they were sorry, when in fact it would have been a golden example of it. The last time I talked to Henry, he was looking for another job. It's not his lack of ownership in the company that troubles him now; ironically, it's a lack of confidence in his employers' humility.

I'm going to take a pause to make a special note here for other women entrepreneurs. As women, it seems to be in our DNA to say "I'm sorry," and that's good. However, I, as well as many women I know, tend to say "I'm sorry" for everything. When we say it too much, it loses its meaning. We can't be sorry for everything, or no one listens when we say it. So we all, women and men, need to find beauty in the balance between a powerful and a pitiful "I'm sorry."

If you think you're sharing your vulnerabilities with those you work with, make sure that's true. Ask them questions that get at their perception of your vulnerability, things like: Do you think I would tell you if I were worried about X? Do you think that I understand the challenges you're having? People seem on edge, what's happening? How am I contributing to it? Have I shared how I feel about the situation? Do people believe that I really do feel that way, or is there some mistrust? As Brené Brown recommends, say: "Here is the story I have in my head. Is that consistent with your story?" Do I seem to take ownership of my own screwups and properly apologize? Do I accept others when they make mistakes and help them to get better?

Be a Humble Student

Janessa was a JD-MBA from Stanford who'd previously worked as a consultant. She called me one day and explained that what she wanted most in her next job was to work for a good manager and mentor. Although I get asked by countless entrepreneurs for contacts and introductions, I was happy to support Janessa after just one call, and introduce her to whomever she needed to meet. Why? She was pursuing her job search with the humility needed to be great. Instead of looking at the prize at the end—the big title, the money—she looked at the next important step on her journey as learning and growing. In other words, she wanted to continue to be a student. It's a fantastic approach for an entrepreneur, an aspiring leader, and a person.

Contrary to popular understanding by entrepreneurs, we do not have to know everything. We need to be humble and willing to listen and learn—things we are not historically great at. But if we have humility, we can better welcome the knowledge that other entrepreneurs, advisers, board members, teammates, and business partners have to give—and not just about the nuts and bolts of building a company, but also about how to prepare for and manage the intensity of the journey.

At the most fundamental level, as an entrepreneur you need to be a student of your business and acknowledge that you don't know everything about it. You need to be humble enough to listen to the feedback from the market, and to evolve if necessary. You have to employ the mind-set of experimentation. The experimenter doesn't go into a test saying, "I know the answer!" Rather, she goes into it saying, "I have an idea what the answer is, a hypothesis, but I need to test it." The entire enterprise must come from a place of humility in order to work, or at least in order to save you some heartache.

Will Rosenzweig, whom I talked about in chapter 1, told me about one of his students who, after going through a course of study with his business, decided he needed to shut it down. The student wasn't ashamed—he even wrote a blog post about it. "It was a great outcome," said Will. "He employed the tools we taught him about prototyping and customer interviews, and at the end of it he realized he didn't really have a viable solution. He saved himself a lot of time and money and pain and sorrow by running a disciplined process, and 'failing fast' in a way that was a learning experience."

The learning mind-set is critical at the beginning of a career, as it was for Will's student; in the middle, as it was for Janessa; and well into one's career, as it was for Jeffrey Hollander. To this day, Jeffrey puts notes on his computer reminding him of what he wants to be mindful of, and one of those notes reads: *Ask questions, don't provide answers.* "The leader always wants to have the answer," he said. "But every time you come up with the answer is a time that someone else doesn't have the opportunity to."

Share Enough, but Not Too Much

Christine Carter told me there's a very clear line for her about when to show vulnerability and when not to. She shares her mistakes and past scars openly with her clients, even some of her coaching clients who hire her presumably because she's got it all figured out. But, she says, "never publicly expose yourself emotionally on an issue that you haven't processed yourself yet. You can tell all the stories about yourself that you want with total confidence and good humor when you've processed it. But if it's still an issue that you're struggling with, don't share it with those who follow you. Let the people who can help you process it see it, but not the people who are following you. Think of yourself as a coach. Don't coach people on things you can't do yourself."

To a large extent, I agree with Christine. When I was struggling because of Blue Sky, it would not have been appropriate for me to come in to the Plum office and announce, "Hey everyone, just so you know, I'm completely losing my mind here." I was in a dark, depressed space, and my leadership wouldn't have inspired anyone were I to have revealed the depth of my vulnerability. Those were conversations I *did* need to have with someone, for my own well-being, but they were best saved for my trusted friends, trusted mentors, and a really good coach or therapist.

That said, it also didn't do any good to hide that there was something very significant going on with me. A startup culture is a close one, and you simply can't wait until you've processed everything before you open up. As an entrepreneur, especially one who works in an open office space, you are exposed all the time. Yes, you can try to have your game face on, and that works to a degree, but not always. Your people may be direct about asking what's going on with you. You can't share every personal or board-level issue—it's not appropriate—but you can be vulnerable without showing everything.

In my case, everyone at Plum could see the cracks, and I had nowhere to hide. I should have said, "Hey, everyone, I'm having some problems in my life outside Plum, and I may not be myself all the time. My emotions might show, I might not be able to completely hide it. I just want you to know because I always try to be real with you." But I didn't say that, either, and people undoubtedly wondered—and worried—about what was going on with me and whether it had something to do with the company.

You can't always anticipate when you'll be in a situation in which an employee or a colleague will ask a hard or a sensitive question. You need to respond, and yet there's no clear line to tell you how. You can choose to be guarded, or choose to be vulnerable. You have to weigh what can be most effective for your leadership. I've learned to always err on the side of vulnerability, because it has the potential to create so much trust.

One example of negotiating this tension well came in the form of a Jeopardy game we played at Plum. As with my time at Clif, there was a moment when Plum was going through a lot of change. At the time, we were considering merging with another company, and if we were to, we would use that company's name as ours. Everyone knew what was going on, and ultimately they knew that Neil and I would make the decision. I had very mixed feelings about a potential merger, and I could tell our people were questioning it, as I was. I wanted to bring everything to the surface without telling them I was having mixed feelings about it. But we needed to create a very transparent way to talk about it. So we created a Jeopardy game board, with everything from "softball questions" to "hardball questions" that the team could throw out to Neil and me. The more hardball the question, the more points they would earn toward a really nice, very foodie-indulgent company lunch. They included things like, "What if we screw up by veering away from what we know best?" or "What if we disappear as a company?" To which we answered, "Look, this is a challenging decision because there are so many factors at play. But here's how we're thinking about it right now." At the time, we were leaning toward the merger. Neil and I shared what we were concerned about personally, but we were also able to be a sounding board to hear our employees' concerns, and at the end of the day we were also able to make our leadership clear. Sharing our fears took nothing away from that. We ended up deciding against the merger, and given the conversations we'd had with our team, we were able to go back and share what we learned, what our people had taught us along the way, and, ultimately, why we had decided against it. It became a moment of bonding versus confusion.

Another example of this tension came recently for me at REBBL. I was talking with a loyal consultant, exploring the possibility of having her come on as a C-level manager. At first she didn't seem to have any interest in it, but then it suddenly became clear that she very much wanted the job, to the point that she mentioned the possibility to the agency she worked for. It seemed that we had gone from zero to one hundred in a moment. I realized I had to slow the conversation down to be able to really vet the implications of the hire for the company. She lived across the country, and we just hadn't determined whether that distance would work. When I said we needed to slow the pace of the conversation, it became an emotional moment and a rather tense phone call.

There was so much more going on beneath the surface of this decision for me. Our headquarters is in Berkeley. I tele-commute from Santa Rosa. Palo is in New Mexico. The ability to work from home is critical to me, and I didn't feel comfort-able drawing a hard line that someone else couldn't do so. And yet we needed to determine what was best for the company in the long run in terms of high-level leaders telecommuting, es-pecially from across the country where there were time zone and travel cost considerations. In short, I felt conflicted. Here was a quintessential vulnerability moment. I had a choice: I could either play very cool and professional with this woman, and be guarded. This would look something like letting her know we would decide and get back to her. I could just drag my feet on the conversation, since she didn't want to make the transition for about six months. From a leadership point of view, she wouldn't know the degree to which we were uncer-tain. But it would have left her feeling unsettled and it would have compromised trust between us. I'm highly conscious of how rotten it feels on the receiving end of uncertainty.

I chose vulnerability instead. I called her and said, "I want to have a very transparent conversation. Here's the thing—I really care about you, and you're doing some incredible things for this company." I specifically listed the areas that I thought she was doing great in, so she'd know I wasn't just blowing smoke. "But I want to make sure you're clear on the challenges we have to work out over a period of time before we could hire you, and they're challenges that may get in the way of ever hiring you. It may be too challenging to have all C-level staff telecommuting, and the fact that you live on the East Coast may make this too hard. But I have mixed feelings on the matter. I feel like a hypocrite, because I'm a CEO who's telecommuting. In an ideal world, I'd be in the office each day, but I can't be. Part of me thinks we're doing pretty well this way. But the question remains whether it's the best way to set up the company long-term. That's what we all need to think about." She shared with me how much she appreciated my willingness to be transparent. We ended the conversation with a commitment to always be open, and I felt like it took our relationship to a new level of trust. It was such a poignant reminder to me about what we, our people, and our company gains when we focus on being human.

I've said before that love belongs in everything we do. And if love belongs in everything we do, so then does courage. It takes courage to love what you do, because it hurts so much when you fail. Those who have bold humility will lean into that failure, share it, learn from it, and move on. And then they'll be the ones whom other entrepreneurs come to when they falter and need a little lift. That faltering—even free-falling—is the subject of the next, and I believe the most critical, chapter.

CHAPTER 10

Staying Sane in the Fast Lane

The Entrepreneur's Physical and Emotional Well-Being

W hen I was a kid, I raced everywhere at top speed. One afternoon when I was seven, I dashed to the refrigerator, grabbed a gallon of milk, and instead of carefully pouring it into a glass for my after-school drink, I spilled it all over the beige linoleum kitchen floor. My mom saw this kind of behavior all the time, and quite early on in my childhood, she justifiably became fed up. If I wasn't spilling food, then I was slamming doors in my rush, talking at breakneck speed, or generally whirling through the house like a Tasmanian devil. I always felt like there was a never-ending amount of exciting things to do, like getting outside to play with my neighbor friends, or actually drinking the milk (getting it got in the way), if I could just get to them faster. During these episodes, my mom would, in her typical pose of exasperation, run a hand through her bleach-blonde and perfectly shaped hair and shout, "Sheryl! You need to slow down!" But slowing down was not part of who I was.

I was equally intense in school, and I would hold myself to ridiculous standards. I had a teacher who was inclined to give me an A+++ on occasion, and so if I got only an A+, or, god forbid, an A, I was distraught. What had I done wrong? Could I fix it or make it better somehow? I'm not sure where it all came from, other than this intense drive for perfection. In hindsight, I realize that I must have been a pretty exhausting kid to be around.

My energy was boundless. When I was in high school, I worked at the Pickle Barrel deli, the local staple for people who craved authentic Jewish deli food, like rugelach and rye bread. I'd go to work on Friday right after school, stay until closing at around eleven, and then work from opening until four p.m. on Saturday and Sunday, too. And, even with those hours, I didn't sacrifice my social life, and usually went out with friends after work, partying as hard as I worked. During the week, it was back to the books. It was all out at all times. I kept the same pace in college at the University of Michigan, alternating working hard and playing hard—the point was to do everything to the absolute limit, to the A+++ level. My goal was never to slow down. For fuel, all I needed was affirmation from others, be it an A+ on a term paper or a high five after showing up in the morning to drink beer before a football game after having partied the whole night.

I'm far from the only entrepreneur with a hard-charging personality—it's how most of us are wired. Entrepreneurs *have* to be driven in order to want to take on such a job, and in order to succeed at it. But as the saying goes: "Your greatest strength can also be your greatest weakness." Because what do you think happens when you take someone who is not prone to self-care, who gets laser focused, who is used to facing ten people's worth of work and getting it done and then some, and put that person in a scenario where the stakes are high, where the workload is truly unmanageable, where there is little about the outcome he or she can control, and where no one is giving him or her a "job well done," let alone an A++? What do you think happens when this person faces failure, probably for the first time, as he or she almost inevitably will? It seems like a recipe for a crash, and it is.

If You Do X, Then Y Will Happen

I ran Plum the way I always did everything: with great intensity. But it was unlike any other endeavor I'd ever taken on.

In the early days of Plum, when we were still called the Nest Collective, we were looking to buy a small company that we could grow through innovation. Revolution Foods seemed a perfect fit—it was a company committed to changing the face of school nutrition, both through the schools themselves and through offering healthy lunchbox options. Kirsten and Kristen (whom I talked about earlier in this book) were deeply passionate people, and Neil and I clicked with them from the moment we met them. I led a deal with Revolution Foods to license their name; we wanted to create an innovative consumer products brand that would change the face of the lunch box. It was a tricky negotiation, and due to its complexities and long-term implications, I included our wicked-smart lawyer, Tim, in the negotiation strategy and, of course, in the legalities. A good deal with Revolution Foods was critical—it was like marrying someone, and we needed to make sure we did everything right, to make sure we could capture the value we'd created in the brand. Tim added huge value to the deal, yet his bill at the end was $180,000. I was horrified. We didn't have that kind of money. I should have been more on top of the multiplying hours. It was my fault—I berated myself for it and felt embarrassed and ashamed as I shared the news with our investors. I grinded on it at night. I forced myself to move on, but little did I realize that I was chipping slowly away at my self-worth. It was like I'd gotten an F on that assignment.

There were other tough grades ahead. Also in the very early days of Plum, I thought we'd see an immediately fast trajectory like I'd experienced with Luna, not appreciating the support system I'd had at Clif—one that included strong retailer relationships, a team of five salespeople, an established broker network, and experienced marketing and product-supply-chain teams. We didn't hit our numbers, I thought I was such an idiot for my naïveté, and one of our investors, Glen, reinforced my feelings of shame by telling me that I hadn't thought through it well. (Even though, to be fair, forecasts are notoriously difficult in startups.) Chip, chip at my self-worth.

Another hard moment for me was when a retailer that we really wanted to take our products said they wouldn't appeal to his shoppers. I was playing the role of head of sales and, well, the *only* employee in sales at the time. I racked my brain—what was I doing wrong if I couldn't convince this retailer, who had women as his primary shopper, to pick up a line of baby food? I felt like there was a sign on my head saying "I suck at this."

For two years there wasn't a single moment of calm—it all just ratcheted up and up and up. The early days of Plum seemed fanatical in terms of work pace, but mind-numbingly slow in terms of progress.

Every development brought more and more conflict, and required more and faster decision-making. And true to form, I couldn't shrug any of it off. Intense people don't shrug things off and say, "Whatever! It'll all be fine, just chill." I've gotten much better over the years at moderating my intensity, and I know now that most businesses have nine lives, but the point is, I'll *never* be chill. If an investor seemed dissatisfied, I ruminated over and over the issues all evening, wondering what I could do to make it better. If a buyer wanted something, I was going to move heaven and earth to make it happen if I could. Every issue, from the color of the walls of our office to the ingredients we put into the food we made, felt crucial because it represented our brand, our values—it was us. In the process, I was grinding my teeth off in pieces and my hair was slowly turning gray. I had headaches every day for about six straight months at the end of my tenure.

I was used to fast-paced—most of my life had been lived in a high-speed zone—but this was so fast it felt like there was nothing I could do to keep up. As soon as I put out a fire— brokers who weren't performing, running out of product because we couldn't get packaging fast enough to keep up with demand, investors wanting to see their return on investment— another would emerge. Not only that, but I had to do all this while raising outside money to keep up with our growth. I had two full-time jobs, running the business and raising money. It was like running uphill with no breath and no time to stop and catch it. What's more, I was used to a certain formula working: apply yourself, put in your time and energy, and eventually you will see results. "If you do x, then y will happen": this is the mantra of the overachiever, of the Little Engine That Could. Not so with an entrepreneurial foray. It felt so out of my control; I couldn't make money through willpower, or keep obstacles at bay for more than a few hours despite my constant attention. I worried that my reputation would be ruined—not to mention my self-image—if this company failed.

So why did I stay? Why didn't I just say, "This is a bit too much, and I'd like my life back, please." Well, because I loved it. Because the highs were unlike anything I'd ever experienced in business. For instance, we hired a young, talented packaging designer, Rachel, who, with Neil's creative direction, came up with stunningly beautiful designs that made our packages look exquisite. Our research and development guru, Molly, had the discipline and know-how of a food scientist balanced with the palate of a gourmet restaurant–level chef. She developed new products that met our high standard of nourishment with such yummy taste that they not only made babies smile, but caused moms to add them to their purses as snacks for themselves. I was incredibly proud of the work we were doing at Plum, and of the people who were doing it. Even athletes were using Plum for a burst of organic energy. The hard work was beginning to pay off, and our sales started to soar after about a year and a half. Both Glen and another investor, Bill, announced at their annual dinner with the heads of the companies they invested in that Plum was becoming the crown jewel of their portfolios. It was a dream come true. We birthed a baby and, like adoring parents, Neil and I were astonished by its growth in the world.

And so I stayed. And I worked. And I worried, and churned, and retained my role of chief firefighter. I kept riding the roller coaster.

The tumultuous ride might have been enough to put me over the edge on its own. But it was only the half of it. Patrick was still dealing with the emotional fallout from Blue Sky, and I was dealing with Patrick.

I'll never forget my alarm clock going off at six a.m. after a night of staring at the ceiling while work issues swirled around in my head. Patrick, who historically would have popped right out of bed and gotten the coffeepot going, barely stirred. He'd been up all night, as he had been for the past month. It had gotten so bad that he had started to go to the Stanford Sleep Medicine Center to learn how to sleep again. After that alarm rang he grabbed me in a tight hug, not wanting to let go, to ward off what the effort of another day closing his company would entail. I pulled away from his embrace to get ready for the day, wanting nothing more than to stay there with him, to help him find his feet. He was severely depressed, feeling the weight of responsibility for losing our savings and taking Blue Sky's failure personally. For our eleven years of marriage, he'd been a rock, and now he wasn't, and he needed me to be that solid ground.

I tried to be there for him; I wanted to be there more than anything. But I had to get our kids ready for the day, packing their lunches and making sure their shoes were tied all while trying to shield them from our stress. Then, after getting the boys to school, I had to refocus, so that I could crank out the work at Plum.

In retrospect, it's easy to see that something had to give. My life felt out of control, all the time, but I believed I had to keep a strong facade—for Plum's investors, for the employees, for Neil, for Patrick, for my two boys. All that hard-charging energy that had fueled me for so long now swirled around in a pressure cooker of stress, and I was cooked to the point of exploding but was too busy taking care of others to realize it.

I'd always been an active person—running, cycling, and hiking at every opportunity. And I'd habitually been a healthy eater, but, like many women, I frequently wanted to lose just a few pounds. I wasn't really trying to diet, but one day I noticed that my weight had dropped after a period of light eating and heavy exercising to relieve the stress. Patrick and I had taken a vacation to Maine, trying to decompress from Blue Sky, but Patrick was getting enraged calls from creditors. My only respite was to run, so I ran for two hours so I could face the fallout when I met up again with Patrick. After that, the running didn't stop. People started commenting on my weight loss, which appealed to me, as I thought, *How nice, they noticed. I must be doing something right.* I kept it up and watched as the numbers on the scale dipped lower and lower, and with that as incentive, I continued to step up my exercise regime.

Suddenly it wasn't enough to run for an hour a day anymore. I needed to run for two hours one day a week, then two days, then each and every day. I would come in to the office a little late in order to exercise—a sure sign, I felt, that I was prioritizing my health.

My diet consisted of blueberries in the morning, blueberries and cottage cheese in the afternoon, and a big bowl of steamed vegetables for dinner. The running continued, the numbers got lower, and I was satisfied. The numbers on the scale came to represent so much more than my weight. Being disciplined about the type of food I ate and amount of exercise I got was something I could manage. They were a handle on my life, proof that I could accomplish a goal, proof that I was in control. My weight was the one thing that held to my favorite formula: "If you do x, then y will happen." I ate less and exercised more, and my weight dropped. Not only that, but I was getting what I perceived to be the external approval that I was doing at least *something* right. Just like getting A's in school.

And this is how I developed anorexia. I've always had the tendency to push, push, push, and now this trait was expressing itself in its most dangerous form. It was destined to come to the surface when faced with a period of great stress and unpredictability.

What Entrepreneurs Have in Common with Air Traffic Controllers

My former Stanford colleague Professor Baba Shiv studies the emotional brain and its role in shaping decisions. I asked him why more studies haven't been conducted on the stress responses of entrepreneurs. He said it's because researchers recognize that entrepreneurs fall into the same category of individuals as police officers, air traffic controllers, and people in the military. These jobs involve chronic stress and, notably, a feeling of a lack of control. When you don't feel in control, your cortisol levels are higher, and excess cortisol can result in a shrunken hippocampus—which makes people less capable of managing their emotions. There's also research that shows that in moments when people are stressed, their IQ actually goes down, just at the time you need to be at the top of your game.[*] People in positions of power—like CEOs of established companies, or doctors—

[*]Nicholas Kristof, "It's Not Just about Bad Choices," *New York Times*, June 13, 2015.

often have lower levels of cortisol because they have a feeling of being in control; they know what has worked and not worked, and they can pull the right levers. But entrepreneurs are in a different category. They face a future that is uncertain from one day to the next, building their startup from little more than a vision and a big leap of faith. Put that way, is it any wonder that I developed a disease that is most connected to a desire for control? And is it any wonder that hard-charging entrepreneurs are particularly susceptible to depression, divorce, drug abuse, and suicide? No wonder many say they ended their entrepreneurial experience with post-traumatic stress disorder.

Many other entrepreneurs compromise their health by pushing themselves to the verge of collapse, then using drugs to buoy themselves up—a phenomenon that's getting more and more attention, especially in Silicon Valley. As the *San Jose Mercury News* noted, "With a booming startup culture cranked up by fiercely competitive VPs and adrenaline-driven coders, and a tendency for stressed-out managers to look the other way, illicit drugs and black-market painkillers have become part of the landscape here in the world's frothy fountain of tech."[*]

It seems that our culture thinks of money as a critical resource for our companies, yet forgets that *people are the most essential resource of all!* We must give ourselves the oxygen we need not only to survive through a startup experience, but also to thrive.

I wasn't thriving; I was slowly killing myself. But the brain

---

[*]Patrick May and Heather Somerville, "Use of Illicit Drugs Becomes Part of Silicon Valley's Work Culture," *San Jose Mercury News*, July 25, 2014.

works in such complex ways, especially with anorexia, that if you'd told me I wasn't taking care of myself, I would have wholeheartedly argued the opposite. "Look," I'd have said, "despite how crazy things are at work, I'm still taking the time to care for myself by prioritizing exercise. I'm eating fruits, vegetables, and proteins. I'm *fine*." Never mind that I'd come to hate running but felt bound to it like it was some twisted, self-imposed prison term. Never mind that whenever Friday night rolled around, I'd have a few glasses of wine and, because I was finally able to let down my guard just a little bit, I would binge eat, so desperate was my body for nutrition. (It also led to a cycle in which I felt I had to be even more controlled all the other days.) Never mind that tasks at work that I used to complete fairly quickly now took me twice as long, so weakened was my focus.

Everyone around me could see that I wasn't okay. One afternoon Neil and I drove over the Bay Bridge from Plum's office in Oakland to San Francisco for a meeting. Neil turned to me and said, "We should talk about you and what's going on."

"I've just been really tired lately," I responded, hoping that would end the conversation. I was in work mode and didn't feel like a having a heart-to-heart about whatever it was he was seeing.

But he plowed ahead. "I think you have an eating disorder based on how you look, how you eat, and how you exercise."

"What? That's ridiculous," I said, cutting off the conversation at a moment when, if I'd been willing to do it, if I'd been open to listening to signs that something was wrong, I could have addressed the disease before it got totally out of control. Inside, though, I was actually rejoicing. That other people were noticing my weight loss—the way my clothes hung on my frame, the new sharpness of my cheekbones—meant that it was actually working, that I was accomplishing results. And since I'd always craved affirmation by others (even if, in this case, that wasn't what they were trying to do), this feedback fueled my regimen even more.

Crash Landing

After the Blue Sky implosion, it took about three months before Patrick found his footing again. In hindsight, I realize that his ability to bounce back was pretty remarkable. He recognized what a bad place he was in, and he took the steps he needed to get better. Despite a lifetime of thinking that therapy was a waste, he dove deeply in, he opened up to friends to get support, and he began to forgive himself. Although it was painful, he worked on getting a job to feel productive again. He found the perfect position in innovation at The Clorox Company. He could still be the entrepreneur he always wanted to be, but in a big company with the resources that it takes to bring ideas to life, a healthy P&L, and smart people everywhere. Each day, he felt better and stronger, and he became himself again, only a little more humble and grateful for life.

As Patrick grew stronger, my anorexia got worse. I don't know why—perhaps because some part of me knew I couldn't completely fall apart until he'd gotten better. Or perhaps it was just a slow descent with a multiplicative effect, and I would have ended up there no matter what.

Eventually I had to admit that I wasn't okay, though I didn't really attribute it to my eating. I just knew that something had changed, that I was no longer the unstoppable force I used to be, and that I had little energy and was unable to focus. I would yell at my kids for yelling, the ultimate in irony. I'd burst out in anger at anything that Patrick did that just rubbed me the wrong way. ("You didn't set the table right." "You didn't get all the things from the store that I asked." Sure, it's stuff that couples deal with all the time, but my reactions were way out of proportion.) I was so tense all the time, living on pins and needles. I just couldn't cope, which was very un-Sheryl.

Given all that, after my sixth time raising money for Plum, the last round of financing we'd need to get the company to $100 million and the level for a sale to a strategic buyer, I decided to leave my company baby. Beyond the stress and what had become a sort of chronic grumpiness, I didn't have the stamina for the hours anymore. I missed my sons and was desperate to spend more time with them. I felt like I just didn't have the energy and the grit needed to take Plum to the next level. I knew that our employees, our investors, Neil, and the company's potential deserved more than I could give. I needed to be more focused on my family. Even in my altered state I was smart enough to see it. It was hard to say good-bye to being with my baby Plum every day, but it was more important to me to see Plum thriving in the world from afar. I could leave for a job at Stanford and trust that Neil would run things with an expert hand, which he does to this day.

I'd like to say that with Patrick doing better, and with my days no longer consumed by the never-ending crises at Plum, I was able to see what was really going on with me and seek help. Unfortunately, that was not the case. The seed of anorexia that had been planted while I was at Plum had taken root and grown beyond my control.

Being at Stanford invigorated me, especially as I built a new, long-term, innovative strategic plan for the Center for

Entrepreneurial Studies and hired a new, passionate team. With Professor Chuck Holloway, I developed a new way of teaching entrepreneurship that we coined Stanford Total Venture Design that I was so proud of. Yet I kept right on with my exercising, eating, and hard-charging ways throughout the transition.

It gave me a moment of pause when one of the cofounders of the center, Irv Grousbeck, one of the most revered professors at Stanford and a highly successful entrepreneur, said during my annual review, "Sheryl, you're losing weight at a shocking rate. I'm not sure what's going on, it's none of my business, but I'm worried and I'm here if you'd like to talk about it." He looked at me like I was to be pitied, like I was sick. Patrick, meanwhile, was worried out of his mind about my weight loss. I was beginning to believe that in my desire to be in control, I was losing control.

In June 2013, Plum was sold to the Campbell Soup Company. This was great for Plum, as it would give the investors and our employees a great return and would allow us to get Plum's products to many more kids. For Patrick and me, it was what we needed to get back on our feet financially. Two years into my gig at Stanford, Patrick and I decided to slow our lives down and move to wine country in Santa Rosa. I wanted to commit much more time to the kids. Connor was turning thirteen and Gavin ten, and I wanted to become a daily presence, physically and mentally, in their lives, just as their responsibilities were getting greater in school and sports.

It was in Santa Rosa that everything caught up with me. There I was, living an idyllic life. Our financial pressures had eased. Patrick was happy again. Our boys were thriving, and

I was finally getting to spend more time with them. I'd ostensibly fixed everything that was amiss, yet still something was very wrong—and now I was no longer distracting myself from feeling it. I would walk aimlessly around our house, running the tips of my fingers along the fabric of the couch, the smooth ceramic of a decorative dish, and wonder what the hell I was doing and what the hell was wrong with me. Why was I so sad? Why was I so incapable of making even the smallest, most insignificant decision, like what brand of soap to buy or what book to read, when I had been in charge of so many major decisions for so long? And I had to finally be honest with myself: the numbers on the scale were dipping too low, and it was starting to scare me. I picked up a book written by Portia de Rossi, the actress, who had recovered from anorexia. I was curious because I recognized that there might be something seriously wrong with me. I read that when she was at her lowest point, her numbers on the scale were the same as mine.

And so it was on a quiet March day, when Patrick was at work, the boys were at school, and I was all by myself feeling terrible, scared, and depressed, that I decided to call a therapist and make an appointment. It was the beginning of a very long road back to health. I assembled a new team, not to help me launch a business, but to help me recover. It took a long time before I was able to let go of my compulsion to run so much each day, but with my team's help, I reduced my amount of exercise. I slowly increased my calorie intake. I threw away every scale we owned (and haven't replaced them to this day), and I had new goals—to buy larger-size clothes. A therapist, a nutritionist, Patrick, and a few close friends became instrumental parts of my team, and with their help, I'm doing really well. I've now learned that "you look great" doesn't mean "you look fat." That's huge for me. It takes a very long time to say you're completely "recovered" from anorexia, but I'm healthy and doing better every day.

The Genetic Makeup of Entrepreneurs

Dr. Michael Freeman, the psychiatrist and business coach I referenced in chapter 7, told me that perfectionism like mine is a trait that's associated with a range of anxiety conditions, including anorexia/bulimia, but also obsessive-compulsive personality disorder. And yes, you see it in a lot of entrepreneurs. "People who have compulsivity as a trait tend to be high achievers in general because they finish things," Dr. Freeman said. "And they finish them well, so they get rewarded for them. So it's an example of a self-reinforcing behavior-reward-behavior loop that is highly rewarded economically and in many other ways."

Ah, but there's even more in the crazy cocktail that makes up the entrepreneur. In the book *The Hypomanic Edge*, the psychologist John Gartner argues that hypomania, which is a milder version of mania—may have an entrepreneurial connection. "They're like border collies—they have to run," Gartner told *Inc.* magazine of people with hypomania. "If you keep them inside, they chew up the furniture. They go crazy; they just pace around. That's what hypomanics do. They need to be busy, active, overworking."[9]

Dr. Freeman was the lead researcher on a study titled "Are

---

[9] Jessica Bruder, "The Psychological Price of Entrepreneurship," *Inc.*, September 2013.

Entrepreneurs 'Touched with Fire'?'"* that shed light on the question of entrepreneurs' mental health as never before. In this preliminary study, which is now being replicated, he and his team found that entrepreneurs reported significantly more experiences of having one or more lifetime mental health conditions, or were part of families that had them, than a comparison population. They were also "significantly more likely to report a lifetime history of depression, ADHD, substance use conditions, and bipolar diagnosis" than the comparison group was. In conclusion, the study says that "current findings add to a growing body of work suggesting that mental health symptoms, in individuals and their family members, may co-occur with highly advantageous and adaptive outcomes that benefit both the individual and society." In more straightforward terms, it's like I said at the outset of this chapter: your greatest strength is your greatest weakness.

So what are we to make of this? If intensity plus founding or running a business equals threat to one's health, does that mean that intense people shouldn't be entrepreneurs? Not at all. Health trouble is not a foregone conclusion, as long as we pay attention to what's happening with us and get help when we need it. It's the dirty secret that entrepreneurs don't talk about. MBA programs don't pay enough attention to the darker side of entrepreneurship, even though they could really make a difference because their faculty members could be studying the issue in more depth. Dr. Freeman said he thinks MBA programs are allergic to mental health.

*Michael A. Freeman, M.D., et al. "Are Entrepreneurs 'Touched with Fire'?" Pre-publication manuscript, April 17, 2015. http://www.michaelafreemanmd .com/Research_files/Are%20Entrepreneurs%20Touched%20with%20 Fire%20(pre-pub%20n)%204-17-15.pdf.

"I had this amazing experience probably about four or five years ago," he said. "I gave a talk to the faculty of Stanford business school, and I was talking about bipolar disorder and hypomania and the connection between hypomania and entrepreneurship. . . . When we got to the discussion section, the faculty said, 'You just described one-third of our MBA students.' I said 'That's great, because right across the street is the Stanford Medical Center Department of Psychiatry. Why don't we diagnose all your MBA students?'" Such a thing would never happen, Dr. Freeman knew. "They attach so much stigma and shame [to mental health]. They don't even want to know what the mental health profiles of these people are."

Emotional Check-Ins

We need to cast light on the issue of entrepreneurial mental health, and we need to find healthy ways to make sure the pressure doesn't build up. We need to nurture ourselves and get support throughout our startup experience, so we and our companies have the greatest chance of reaching our full potential. To begin with, we need to meditate. I know, I know— this is starting to sound as rote as your mom telling you to eat your veggies. Study after study shows that meditating lowers stress levels. Research demonstrates that in as little as eight weeks, meditating causes the areas of the brain that control stress to get larger and be better able to handle it.° Studies also show that reduced stress levels lead to higher intelligence

° Brigid Schulte, "Harvard Neuroscientist: Meditation Not Only Reduces Stress, Here's How It Changes Your Brain," *Washington Post*, May 26, 2015.

and better decision making.* Professional athletic teams are now teaching their players to meditate to accentuate peak performance. So there is good reason that the advice to do it is becoming ubiquitous.

Vanessa Loder, a friend whom I met while I was serving on the Zuke's natural pet treats board, left the intensity of the private equity world to find her calling. Vanessa is now the founder and CEO of Akoya Power and cofounder of Mindfulness Based Achievement, which she calls the "new MBA." Its purpose is "to empower and inspire millions of women by teaching them how to shift from overwhelm to ease." When she started, she sent a note around to her network, challenging them to participate in a five-minute meditation moment each day for thirty days through Akoya's website. The idea was to just stop, sit, and breathe. I'll admit, I started off thinking, "This is annoying and it's going to feel like forever." (Remember, I'm the kid who couldn't even wait for a glass to pour my milk into.) What I found was that those five minutes slowed me down and recentered me, and afterward I was better able to separate my tasks instead of doing them all at once. I was able to work more efficiently because I was able to unwind the knots I was getting myself into while I was multitasking.

Even if you meditate regularly, you are not truly taking care of yourself if you don't get great medical care. Would an athlete skip the doctor? Of course not, and neither should you, no matter how busy you are. The demands on an entrepreneur *are* physical (maybe it's not football, but in many ways, it can

* Barbara Isanski, "Under Pressure: Stress and Decision Making," *Observer* Vol. 23, No. 6. July/August 2010. Association for Psychological Science. http://www.psychologicalscience.org/index.php/uncategorized/under-pressure-stress-and-decision-making.html.

feel like a contact sport!) as well as mental—someone needs to be checking in with you along the way.

On that note, get a professional to help ease your *mind*, too. Therapists and coaches who work specifically with entrepreneurs are becoming more and more common. They can offer you much-needed relief and tools to cope with the stressors around you. As Jeffrey Hollander said, "I'll always be a relatively good customer of my therapist because I know there's always more I have to learn. I never feel I've learned all I need to know about having a healthy relationship to my work."

One of the ways Jeffrey encouraged healthier habits in himself was by making one of Sustain's objectives to create the best working experience that anyone had ever had. "In order to fulfill that goal," he said, "we had to be concerned about creating a healthy workplace. The reality is that if I wasn't modeling that behavior, no one was going to believe that it was what was valued by the company. Saying that you don't want people working twelve hours a day when the CEO is working twelve hours a day is just not credible." He had to unlearn a lot of unhealthy habits, he said, and create more boundaries.

Next, check your energy. Are you on full throttle? Again, to return to the athlete analogy, imagine you're running a marathon. Do you have enough fuel to get you through it, even if—or when—the finish line moves? Because one thing is certain: it will. You must, and I mean *must*, take time to rest and recover, and so must your employees. Make recovery a regular part of your company culture.

Finally, chart your highs and lows. Are you living on a roller coaster, or in a rolling countryside? If the first diagram that comes to mind has dramatic peaks and valleys, you have a problem. You may burn out, you may not, but what's clear is that *something* will give. An investor in Plum, Jed, once told me, "Entrepreneurship is like a roller coaster. Make sure you don't ride the ups and downs hard. Learn how to even out the ride." I interpreted this as, "Don't ride the lows too low," as in, "Don't get too down about things like cost overages and lost accounts." But this investor also meant not to get overly high when the roller coaster goes up. Those big ups and downs will burn you out, because it takes so much energy to recalibrate. Simply being aware of when you're out of the neutral zone goes a long way toward helping even out the ride. Calm down. Notice what's going on in your body. Pace your emotional energy. Meditate, exercise, sleep, talk to a friend, volunteer at a charity. Do what you have to, to stay level.

Second Wind

My friend Greg, a typically affable, fun guy, founded a transportation company. I watched his personal disintegration—and ultimate recovery—from close range. All you had to do was glance at Greg to know he wasn't well (ironically, you could have said the same thing about me). His weight shot up unusually quickly. His complexion, while always susceptible to redness if he got embarrassed or had too many beers, was now red all the time. He was never still, not for a second. You'd get anxious in his presence, because his eyes were always moving, his hands always fidgeting, his body never settled.

Unlike me, Greg was very forthcoming about his stress. "I can't stop looking at my email constantly all day, all night," he said. "What if a driver runs into trouble? I *need* to be on—the stakes are just too high. My drivers and my customers depend

on me, so I *need* to be available 24/7." Greg's wife was fed
up with his hours and his complete lack of focus on anything
except his work. They had four children, whom Greg never
spent time with, and if he did, he was thinking about work. "I
can't do this anymore," he said, shaking. I truly feared he was
going to have a nervous breakdown or a heart attack. And he
was just thirty years old.

Greg had lost all perspective, and he needed to get it back.
Just as I looked for refuge in Santa Rosa, Greg sought quiet,
too. He needed to break the cycle of panic and anxiety that
kept him tethered to his phone. In his case, it wasn't that Greg
didn't have enough control—it was that he felt he had too
much of it, and that if anything went wrong, if a vehicle ran
into trouble, he had to be available.

For plenty of entrepreneurs in his position, that never-
ceasing anxiety wreaks havoc with their brains, and depression ensues. Depression was the number one mental health
condition entrepreneurs reported in Dr. Freeman's study.[*]
Depression accounts for the loss of so many great business
minds, from Austen Heinz, who founded Cambrian Genom-
ics, to Ilya Zhitomirskiy, of Diaspora. The list goes on. Sean
Percival was publicly open about his depression after his
startup failed and welcomed depressed entrepreneurs to get
in touch with him; he was inundated with over five hundred
emails.[†]

---

[*]Michael A. Freeman, M.D., et al. "Are Entrepreneurs 'Touched with Fire'?"
Pre-publication manuscript, April 17, 2015. http://www.michaelafreemanmd
.com/Research_files/Are%20Entrepreneurs%20Touched%20with%20
Fire%20(pre-pub%20n)%204-17-15.pdf.

[†]Biz Carson, "There's a Dark Side to Startups, and It Haunts 30% of the World's
Most Brilliant People," *Business Insider*, July 1, 2015.

Fortunately, this was not Greg's path. He sold his company and took some time to get healthy. He took care of his body again, and he lost the weight he'd gained. He reconnected with his family and grasped the way that being with them filled him up, like much-needed oxygen after a deep dive. He recognized that he and his business were not in fact one in the same.

Greg started working for the new owners of the company and no longer felt that the weight of responsibility was all on him. He was then able to see with clear eyes and an open mind what they were doing wrong. He recognized that he could do better. He recognized that he was really *good* at what he did. He had a new perspective, one that recognized the importance of safety to his business, yet saw how he could handle it in a calmer, more confident way. He wanted to buy the company back and try again.

It was a difficult decision for Greg. But at what personal cost? It would mean he was risking the new, calmer, financially sound life he'd found to go back into the den that had caused so much stress. The bottom line was that he really wanted to try it, and he felt he could manage the stress better the second time around. With his wife's blessing, he went for it and bought his company back. But he did things very differently this time. He set clear limits on his availability. He hired more help and found people he trusted and he could delegate to with confidence. He invested time and money into working with a business coach to help him stay on track. He continued to prioritize not only his time with his family, but also his health. He learned how to be vigilant about focusing on safety without having to be on email or the phone 24/7. In fact, he learned that it's *impossible* to be vigilant if you're physically and mentally exhausted. He also understood that he didn't and couldn't control every outcome.

The last time I saw Greg, he was killing it. The company was doing incredibly well, and he was justifiably proud—he was as proud of his professional accomplishments as he was of his ability to actually have fun with his work and to be more grounded with his family. It was not the burden it once had been, perhaps because he knew that if he had to let go, it would be okay. He was not his company. The point is, he'd found the sweet spot, the *joy*, in entrepreneurship. When he was able to take care of himself, he didn't feel like the house was going to cave in with every step he took.

I had a second wind much like Greg's, and I've already talked a lot about what led me to REBBL—how it sparked my passion, how I had long talks with Patrick in order to gain his buy-in. Most important, like Greg, I'm managing the ups and downs differently this time around. I prioritize my health and my family above all, and I listen to those who tell me I need to check myself. I set priorities for my team, and every day I work on making really clear decisions while still getting the wisdom of the talented people around me. I love REBBL, but my self-worth doesn't rise and fall based on the kind of day or week I've had. I am clear about the boundaries I've set with those who could otherwise have an unhealthy influence on me. I set a very clear "no assholes" rule with investors and employees, and that means that I've set the bar high for colle-giality and kindness. I now have the confidence to reinforce it. I can get excited and joyful, and also frustrated and mad, but I've learned to see it with more of a "third eye" and don't get as affected by it all. Importantly, I have the energy needed to run a company again. I feel happy and confident in what I'm doing.

The point is, when things were bad, neither Greg nor I had healthy ecosystems. We'd let the temperature rise too high, and as the ground melted beneath our feet, we began to sink. We had to find solid ground again and rebuild from the bottom up.

I'm much better at leaning inward now, and it's my most common advice to entrepreneurs. Before you insist you're feeling great, ask: *Am I really taking care of myself?* You know the true answer to this question, even if you don't want to admit it. The mind can play tricks on us, though, and not just in the case of an illness like anorexia. This is why you must be very disciplined—something you are probably already very good at—about removing distractions. Focus on whether you are well, or not. Know that your company, your family, and your life are at stake.

I've found, through my own experience and through the insight of others, that it is possible to maintain your sanity in the fast lane—you just have to be diligent about it. And since, if you're an entrepreneur, you are mighty skilled at working hard, this self-care project could be easy if you invest the same energy into it as you do everything else. Just put your wellness—yourself—in the number one slot on your list of priorities.

CHAPTER 11

The Graceful Good-Bye

The Entrepreneur and Letting Go

E very entrepreneurial venture has an exit door. It can look like an ambling ramp, or a well-lit pathway. It can look like an emergency exit, or even an Eject! button. But there *is* an exit. You may never want or need to use it, but you should know where it is and what it looks like.

In the beginning, leaving is the last thing you're thinking about. You're just trying to breathe life into the startup and are looking toward where you want it to go. As it grows and becomes a real company, though, it's time to start thinking about what you want the future to look like—for your company and for yourself. If an exit is on the horizon—even if it's far off in the distance—you can start to prepare for it psychologically. That being said, the route from beginning to end is not a straight line. It rises and drops (just as our careers do), and it's important to listen carefully to the whisper in your head that says, "Time to move in this direction." If you really, really listen hard, you'll hear it. If you have only one plan, then you won't hear it. It's amazing to me when I talk with students and they think their career path will go from A to B to C. Any career, especially one of an entrepreneur, is really a circuitous path that goes A, no B, back to A, over to K, oh, better double back to C.

Two of the hardest things about being an entrepreneur are knowing when it's time to let go, and having the courage to do it. Perhaps the venture has outgrown you. Or perhaps *you* have outgrown the venture, and it's time for you to move on to different priorities. To say this decision is an emotional one is an understatement—it's gut-wrenching. At times like this, it's hard to see that there is even a world outside the one that you created and have been deeply immersed in. Sure, you've dealt with uncertainty within the company for ages, but the uncertainty on the outside is terrifying. How can you find something else that you love that much? How can you work for someone else, if that's what option you think is best, when you're used to being the visionary and the leader? You try to take a peek, but it's just blackness.

Once you've decided it's time, the journey has really just begun, because then you must determine how to leave—and I mean that in the logistical sense and in an emotional sense. Whether you have control of the transition or not, the decisions you make have lasting effects. Do you walk out the door with your team in tears, cheering you on to your new life, your investors and board patting you on the back, saying, "Wow, thank you for what you've done for us"? Do you scorch the earth and leave in a ball of fire, with your finger telling them all where to go? Do you let go little by little, until you're just barely hanging on?

And then you're gone. It's a huge life change, it's not a mere switch of jobs. It may be full of joy, regrets, sadness, and rejection. It may be all of these and more. I grieved for Plum. I didn't want to see Neil or even hear about him for a while. It was too painful. Signs of Plum made me feel a sense of loss, and I knew I had to keep my eyes looking forward. But it got even worse than just cutting off reminders of Plum. There was a night when I was out for dinner with my family. I looked around and it was clear that everyone was enjoying themselves. It's like I was watching them from above but not able to engage with them. I felt terrible. I was too despondent to enjoy my family in the way I wanted to. My self-worth was still completely wrapped up in the company that I was no longer a part of.

You need to know how to manage your emotional health through the change, and how to prepare those in your life for the fact that leaving your company, while you may feel like it's the right choice, is still a huge loss. I mourned leaving both Clif and Plum because I loved them both so much, even though, in both cases, I was ready to leave. How do you not only navigate this change, but also use it as an opportunity to grow and thrive? A transition like this can be daunting and challenging, but it can also be thrilling and the best thing that has ever happened to you.

When to Go

Though leaving Plum was difficult, knowing that it was time to go wasn't. I had loved coming in the front doors of what will always fondly be Nest to me. Our original building was small and green, shaped like a diamond, on the split between Emeryville and East Oakland. I loved hearing the sound of my shoes on our wood floor when I walked in, and I loved walking by each person's desk to say hi. I'd greet Bentley, Rachel, Molly, Kory, Sangita, and Neil—people whom I so adored and admired. It warmed my heart to know that they were working so hard, pouring their souls into making Plum thrive. Just pulling into the parking lot energized me. Over time, the team grew. We moved into a beautiful two-floor space, designed to the nines with ample glass and light. We had lots of investors, very important retail accounts, and VPs, directors, and managers. And as the company evolved, so did I. Slowly, little by little, that feeling of bliss vanished. In its place, I felt queasy and sad. I didn't want to go inside the building. The work felt like drudgery instead of fun. I was tired, I missed my kids, and though I didn't have a firm handle on what was going on with my health, I knew something was wrong with me. When I imagined waking up and not having to go to Plum, I was filled with an enormous sense of relief.

There are some who might say, "Every business has its bumps, every job has good days and bad days. Why didn't you just wait it out?" I knew I couldn't. It was different than the usual, "Gosh, I've had a rough couple of weeks!" This feeling didn't go away, didn't even subside. I felt worse with each passing day, not better. And worst of all, I worried I was hurting the business I loved so much. I felt so low and I didn't want that lowness to rub off on anyone. I was always Sheryl the Cheerleader, not Sheryl the Downer. Plum didn't need me that way.

When I saw an opportunity to work for Stanford GSB's Center for Entrepreneurial Studies, I felt that the job was made for me, and at just the time I desperately needed it. I had always had in the back of my mind that I'd love to work in academia somehow. I always had these fantasies of walking onto a sunny campus, looking up at the historic buildings where so many people began to set the foundation of their futures. I wanted to ponder the biggest questions, the ones that may not have an answer, the ones no one said there *had* to be an answer to. I had always dreamed of immersing myself with students who were energized by having the whole world in front of them. I knew I couldn't leave an all-consuming experience like the one I'd had at Plum without moving on to something that excited me, especially something so new and different. I still wanted to feel like I was part of the game— and all the better if that game had a totally different type of scorecard.

When I told Patrick about Stanford, I felt my same old enthusiasm bubble up again. I felt a bit of myself come back. I told him about meeting Chuck and Irv, who would become my bosses and mentors, and how excited I was by their vision. I shared how the sun shined into the Center for Entrepreneurial Studies, just like the sun shined in the fantasy I'd always had of an academic future. Each day that I thought about the opportunity, waiting to find out if I would be offered the job, I became more thrilled about the prospect. That's how I knew it was time to leave Plum, and I knew it with every fiber of my being.

We've talked about the identity piece of a startup throughout this book, but perhaps it never feels so poignant as when you are preparing to say good-bye. Mark Rampolla, the founder of Zico Coconut Water, was aware from the beginning of the challenge it would be to let go, and he planned for it. "I wanted to commit a decade to the company but didn't intend to commit longer. It was always helpful to keep that in mind. I was also clear that I would do what was right for the business—if it was good for me, and good for my family, and good for the business, then I'd stay. But I always said to [my wife] Maura and my investors, 'Please don't let me be the last one to know if I'm not the guy to take the business to the next stage.'" When the time came for Zico to "go off to college," Mark said he was emotionally prepared because he'd been readying for it for ten years. "I looked at where the business was," he said. "There was a good chance that Coke was going to buy it, and it would be integrated into their system." This had been an ideal scenario from the beginning, he said: that a company like Coke would use its scale and abilities to get a product as healthy as Zico into the hands of consumers. "I realized that for Zico to really win within the Coke system, they've got to love it and treat it as their own," Mark said. "They can best do that if someone within [Coke] is running it. It was not my best and highest use to take it from where it was to a billion-dollar brand. I'm really good at the earlier stage, I love the earlier stage. Now there were other things I wanted to do than just build Zico." If Coke hadn't been interested, or if it had been the best thing for Mark, for the company, and for his family to stay, Mark would have. But the answer became very clear that the time was right to go.

Patrick Meiering, who founded the natural dog snack brand Zuke's, says that it was a spark that led him to found the company, and it was a spark that told him it was time to go. "It's being very real with yourself and saying, Guess what? I love dogs. I love mountains. I love being outside. . . . What's more powerful than all those experiences? For me it was, I love living this one precious life, and what am I going to do with it? Am I learning, am I growing, am I doing my highest good?" He decided to let Zuke's go "in hopes that the next thing really comes to be." He had carried the germ of the idea for Inhabit—a learning, growth, and transformation center—in his back pocket for two or three years while he was running Zuke's, he said, and he would slowly start pulling it out and looking at it. And then it became so powerful to look at that he was ready to go.

These are all stories of leaving at the right time, and yet many people don't. An entrepreneur friend of mine, Mavis, stayed through her snack company's acquisition by a large corporation. She held on but was so crushed by the weight of the hierarchy, the endless rules, the mind-numbing processes, that she felt stripped of her creativity. It killed her spirit, and she finally left with what she describes as PTSD—and she is not the first entrepreneur to use post-traumatic stress disorder to describe his or her experience. On the whole, Jim Becker had a positive exit from the book company he cofounded and led for decades, but he acknowledges he held on a little too long. Once he'd handed over the reins as president, he worked part-time as a creative director for one of the company's divisions. Though he felt he did some good work in that role, it was clear he needed to make a cleaner break. "It was a flawed structure," he said, "created to accommodate me. It was well intentioned, but I said, 'This needs to stop. You need to have a full-time, fully engaged creative director.'" For the sake of the company, he let go.

There's a common theme here: you have to think about what your business needs, and whether you are the best contributor to meet those needs. That's something that feels very jarring to us, given our ego-driven culture. But if you truly love what you've created, then, just as when parents love their children, you'll know that there is a time to let go. It often happens that while you and your skills were the best thing for the company at its inception and early growth, they're no longer a good fit anymore. Perhaps precisely because of the great job you've done, your company has grown to a point where you don't have the right skill set to take it to the next level. Just as it's frequently said that not all technicians should advance to be managers, not all entrepreneurial CEOs should advance to be big-company CEOs. Ouch! Just the thought of it is painful. This is your brainchild, your baby, your hard work, your sweat and tears. How could it not *need* you anymore?

Allow me to strip away the judgment that screams so loudly around this topic. The hard truth is that what's needed in the various stages of a company require very different behaviors. When Stanford professor Charles O'Reilly and Beth Benjamin, a researcher, were coming up with an entrepreneurial model in 2013, they interviewed entrepreneurs and determined that they operate in a very distinctive environment from ongoing business managers. "Entrepreneurial leaders designing new ventures lead in an extraordinary context marked by uncertainty, ambiguous feedback and minimal resources," they found.[*] The behaviors that increase the chances of the leader's success in this environment include inspiring, innovating, learning, executing, and collaborating. They go on to say that one of the greatest challenges for entrepreneurs is "adapting a founder leader-

---

[*]Beth Benjamin and Charles O'Reilly, "Can Founders Scale? The Eight Challenges to Becoming an Entrepreneurial Leader" (working paper, Stanford University Graduate School of Business, November 2013).

ship style" to what's needed in a company when the work to be done is all about managing scale and process. Some founders successfully make the transition; others don't.

On the flip side, I've seen people who are great managers but absolutely hate being part of an entrepreneurial environment. It's too chaotic and uncertain. There are few processes to rely on, and everything feels messy. Perhaps they're well-versed in best business practices and feel they can add value by implementing them, but best practices may not be workable in the early phase that the company's in. They create too much process too early, the company grinds to a halt, and the troops revolt. Hopefully they realize themselves that the fantasy of entrepreneurship doesn't work for them in reality, and they move on to a company where they can thrive.

My point is, there's nothing wrong with the entrepreneur and there's nothing wrong with the manager. Each has an environment in which she thrives; each has an environment that tears out her heart. Instead of attaching unhelpful judgments, instead of berating ourselves for being failures, stupid, or incapable, let's start to celebrate where we are capable and to choose the lives we want. We don't need to hold on to a job that doesn't fit, because there is something else that fits us perfectly out there, if we're courageous and if we're open to discovering it.

Andy Rachleff, the former CEO of Wealthfront, was a longtime venture capitalist and colleague of mine at Stanford. With ease and eagerness, he handed over the Wealthfront CEO job to Adam Nash. He told *Pando*'s Sarah Lacy that "I know my limitations . . . I was meant to be a VC. It's a totally different skill set. Being a good VC doesn't mean you are set up to be a good CEO."[*] He gets it. He's very self-aware to say, "Here's where I'm strong, here's where I'm not." And he knows it's better for him, it's better for the company, it's better for everyone going forward.

If you don't leave at the right time, it can be devastating. It's like the athletes—Michael Jordan, Muhammad Ali, Brett Favre—who had the chance to leave (and really leave, not leave-and-return) at the peak of their careers, but didn't. Or like the sitcom that's fresh and hilarious for years but stays on the air too long. We all know what happens when exits are poorly timed, because we've seen it. The athlete limps along while everyone scrutinizes how he's not even a fraction of who he used to be. He's ultimately cut from the team, or not re-signed. The television show gets mocked for having "jumped the shark" and is then canceled. The company founder gets forced out.

Institutional investors know this and actively plan for when the founder needs to leave or be moved into a different role. No one talks about it, but it's true. This doesn't happen so much with venture capital investors, who are generally only going to get involved with a company in the first place if they feel confident that the founder is going to be able to manage it to a better level. Private equity investors, on the other hand, are accustomed to getting their hands much dirtier and having more day-to-day contact with the company. Private equity investors are looking for a surer win and have written a course of action when they decide to invest. Perhaps they intend to

---

[*] Sarah Lacy, "It Doesn't Always End in Tears: Inside Wealthfront's Second Orderly CEO Switch," *Pando*, January 21, 2014, https://pando.com/2014/01/21 /it-doesnt-always-end-in-tears-inside-wealthfronts-second-orderly-ceo-switch/.

keep the founder around for the next stage, but once the company gets to a certain level of scale, they already know they're going to bring someone else on. This doesn't happen each and every time, of course, but it happens a lot. That's why it's so important for you to have a clear vision of your strengths and weaknesses, and to do your research, so that you can write your own story instead of having it written for you.

Step Back

When you're so close to the situation, how can you tell when it's time to go, when you're not helping the business anymore? You need to bring a modicum of objectivity back, and there are two helpful ways to do this. First, though the last time you wrote in a journal might have been in high school, pick up your trusty pen and write—for your eyes only. Write about the stage your company is in. Write what you think it needs. Can it get that from you? If not, is there another place in the company that may be a good fit for your skills? Are you feeling like you need to push yourself into the mix versus naturally being part of it? Why? Think deeply, be honest with yourself. Did you perhaps successfully transition your baby to a new stage in life where it's better cared for by people who thrive in this phase? Are you happy? If not, what's different now than when you were? Are you pining for the "early days" instead of being immersed and joyful in the current moment? Now put the paper aside. Take a break, and pick it up in a day or two. Does what you wrote ring true?

Second—and this exercise can be much more brutal—ask your board to do a performance review for you, even if they haven't initiated it. If you don't have a board or if you don't yet feel ready for that, ask your peers to give you an honest assessment. Ask for notes about your strengths and weaknesses, and how they fit with the needs of the company. Be vulnerable so the company can be strong. They have this assessed, whether you know it or not. Whatever you do, don't react. Ask questions for understanding, but don't get defensive. You won't be able to hear the truth if you're hiding behind a wall, and people will become fearful of sharing their thoughts openly with you. Granted, everyone's judgment is subjective and you can't take every piece of feedback as gospel. But where is the thread of truth you're hearing from others? Where is it resonating with you deep down? Your heart needs to be fully open to welcome this time of learning and growing. You don't need to make a rash or immediate decision. Let it percolate, live with it a bit. Does it start to feel more and more right and true to you? This process probably doesn't sound easy, and it isn't. But chances are good that the truth—whether it indicates you should stay or go—is plain for everyone else to see anyway. Do what Mark Rampolla did, and tell those around you not to let you be the last to know it's time to go. This level of openness can be tough, but it's also very liberating.

A word of caution: there will be employees in your company who won't want to see you go. It's very easy to be submerged in the warmth of that love and admiration. However, that doesn't mean that you should stay. It's important to understand that a transition won't be hard only for you. In a growing company, you are part of a family, with some members who have been with you since the early days (and you have war wounds that you share), and your letting go is scary for many people who are part of it. But if you keep as your guiding light what is best for the company and what's best for you, you will make the right decision.

How to Go

Plenty of advice exists about how to design exit strategies from a legal and financial point of view, and I'm not going to get into that. (You're welcome.) Rather, I want to get above the details and think about the bigger picture. I want to talk about how to leave a legacy that is unmarred by anger, resentment, or regret, and one that instead is characterized by grace and contentment.

There's no question that the financial piece of an exit is a very big piece. And there's no question that money is a loaded topic. It's a very tricky dance. You have to think about what you deserve based on what you've built. You might even have to argue very forcefully to make sure you're advocating for yourself, that you're getting what's important to you. Again, for the women entrepreneurs out there, we are not always great at this. We jump too quickly to thinking it will be fine, that "they'll take care of me." If you don't advocate for yourself, it will be really easy for everyone to walk away having avoided a hard conversation, but you will walk away feeling lousy about yourself. How can you expect others to value you if you don't believe you're worth it yourself? But you also must be reasonable. You must ask, Am I being my best self? Am I serving my values? If I'm saying I feel angry about the money, is that really the truth? Is it really about the money or is it about something else? What do I really deserve? Through all my exits, the way I checked myself was to answer these questions. I also imagined running across the people I worked with again—which I inevitably would. I knew I wanted to be able to look them in the eye again and think, *I handled myself with grace.*

If you don't leave in exactly the manner you'd have chosen (which happens a lot), or with the amount of money you thought was fair, you will undoubtedly feel anger. And then the challenge becomes to let go, to forgive so that you can move forward in a healthy way. Brad Barnhorn, the founder turned investor-adviser, explains it as a way of being in rapport with yourself; you have to think about how your past and your present have led you to this point. "If you believe you never get what you deserve and that people are always looking to take advantage of you," he said, "the potential is high that you'll find yourself having that experience and outcome over and over as long as you let that belief govern your lens of how the world and people treat you." Or, as the psychiatrist and Holocaust survivor Victor Frankl notably wrote, "Between stimulus and response there is space. In that space is our power to choose our response. In our response lies our growth and our freedom."

When you find that space between stimulus and response, it will be easier for you to see the big picture. Everyone's big picture will look different, but mine is very much about relationships. Relationships are paramount to me. I don't want to leave this world feeling that I didn't do my best to nurture and honor the relationships that I have. There are some relationships that haven't lasted, no matter how hard I tried. But in each case, I've always felt like I did whatever is was my power to do, and then I let go. I don't want to be a host to resentments and grudges.

So much of letting go is about ego, and about being aware of its part in your actions. It might even be subconscious, so you have to pay attention carefully in order to keep it in check. This is true when it comes to money, and true when it comes to the act of handing over the reins. One of the trickiest acts for an entrepreneur is choosing or preparing a CEO to take his or her place at the helm. Will they get it? Will they try to make it their own? I can answer those questions: Yes, and yes. And guess what? You *want* them to make it their own.

As a leader, you always have to be looking for talent, whether you need it now or sometime in the future. I am always finding talent to replace me. When I was at Clif Bar, I hired Kevin Cleary, whom I'd worked with at Quaker Oats. Kevin was *outstanding*. And I don't mean he was merely talented, or smart, or creative—I mean he was all these things and more. He was *outstanding*. I made him COO, knowing that I wouldn't be at Clif forever, and that he would be a fantastic replacement. And that's just what's happened.

Neil, too, is outstanding. He is one of the most talented people I have ever met. From practically our first conversation, I knew that I had to hire him at Clif and then start a company with him. He replaced me as CEO of Plum, and he's done an incredible job. I've had moments, though, when I've thought, "Wow, both guys are doing such a great job—I was kind of hoping something would go wrong and people would say 'I wish Sheryl were here.'" It's a really common human inclination, so don't beat yourself up for feeling that way. But do watch it, because it's your ego at work. Patrick Meiering of Zuke's—who now teaches mindfulness—has a particularly refined ego radar. "If I'm in a very egoic space that's 'I did all of this!'—which is completely false, by the way—then it hurts to think I may not be needed." But he points out there's another place the ego rears its head. If a company is doing well without you, he said, "You can [be tempted to] think, 'It's so wonderful that I did all this, and it got it to a point where all the new person had to do was walk in the door.'"

I'm happy to say that my ego is well in check and that those feelings of "you don't need me anymore?" were fleeting; they have long since melted away, vastly overpowered by a feeling of pride in what I *helped* create. To me, the biggest shame would be if I left a company in shambles. This happens with founders all the time. A founder can't get out of the company's way, and takes what he built down with him. Consider Andrew Mason, cofounder and then CEO of Groupon. CNBC's Herb Greenberg named him the worst CEO of 2012.

"Mason's goofball antics," Greenberg wrote, "which can come off more like a big kid than company leader, almost make a mockery of corporate leadership—especially for a company with a market value of more than $3 billion. It would be excusable, even endearing, if the company were doing well (think Herb Kelleher of Southwest Airlines) but it's not. Sales growth is through the floor."°

Sure enough, in early 2013, Mason was fired. In his parting letter to employees he wrote, "After four and a half intense and wonderful years as C.E.O. of Groupon, I've decided that I'd like to spend more time with my family. Just kidding—I was fired today. . . ." He then went on to explain why: "From controversial metrics in our S1 to our material weakness to

---

° Herb Greenberg, "Worst CEO of 2012," CNBC.com, December 18, 2012, www.cnbc.com/id/100320782.

two quarters of missing our own expectations and a stock price that's hovering around one quarter of our listing price, the events of the last year and a half speak for themselves. As CEO, I am accountable. . . . You are doing amazing things at Groupon, and you deserve the outside world to give you a second chance. I'm getting in the way of that." I admire his candor in the end, but it would have been better for him to have stepped out before the damage was done.

How to Grow

Let's say you picked a time to leave your company that you feel great about. It was a productive, even graceful parting of the ways. The money was all sorted, the good-bye parties were heartfelt and meaningful to you. You probably took a well-earned vacation and read novels you'd been meaning to read for years. Now what?

You probably had a plan for what you'd do after, if even only a threadbare plan. Jim Becker and his wife bought a one-way ticket to Europe. Mark Rampolla took some time to think about what he wanted to do and began investing in and advising companies. "I didn't have the need to be the coconut water king for eternity," he said. "I also decided that the opportunity for me was the old adage, close one door and two will open. And the only way those other two will open is when you really close the door. I knew there was a complete unknown. I had zero certainty that I could do it [start a business] again, that I would want to do it again, if I'd be any good at consulting or advising. But I realized I was going to figure it out."

When I left Plum, I had a full-time job at Stanford—my

dream job, in fact. And yet still the transition was excruciating for me. A friend of mine said that when you leave a company, you go through an identity crisis for about a year. You are so used to thinking about your baby nonstop, and even if you've been very careful, your sense of self is affected. I had to have a very clear answer when people asked what I did—when I was at Stanford, and especially afterward, when I didn't have an easy title for a business card. "I serve on boards," I said. I *had* to have an answer. When I first arrived in Santa Rosa, I wanted to meet other people, so I joined a support group of women who gathered regularly in a Unitarian church to talk about whatever was going on in their lives. I had a hard time finding a more formalized group of women to join, so I went for it. They were wonderfully kind people who were in their seventies. As we went around the circle making introductions, each woman explained that she was caring for an ailing husband or parent or spending time volunteering. When it was my turn, I started listing the highlights from my résumé. I was waiting for them to express how impressed they were, but they just sat quietly. All of a sudden I stopped myself and said, "Actually, I'm just trying to find myself again." They all nodded and said, "I think we can help, or at least listen." It felt vulnerable, but it also felt real, and I felt supported. I was a human being. I wasn't a résumé.

Thankfully, I have an incredibly supportive husband who had gone through his own deep sadness. Thankfully, I have wonderful friends who expressed love and concern. And thankfully, we had the money available so that I could take a breath and figure out how to heal, and I could pay for professionals to help me, especially to work through the anorexia that I finally realized I needed to recover from. Most people don't have all those things going for them. What happens to them?

In order to grow through a transition year, you need support. Just as new dads are usually given a checklist to watch for signs of postpartum depression in new moms, those close to entrepreneurs should also have a checklist. The questions would include: Are they sleeping too much? Not enough? Are they engaged with the world? Have there been any changes to their eating patterns? Are they resistant to participating in activities they once loved? Are they talking to friends, to family? Are they able to hold a conversation? Can they talk about anything besides their loss? Look into their eyes: Are they hollow and withdrawn?

Patrick Meiering is one of the most self-aware leaders I've known, and he credits meditation with helping him through his transition. "The moment-to-moment watching of your experience is going to lead you into some deep personal truths," he said. "My favorite phrase when I was agitated was to tell those aspects of myself that always wanted to *do* and be creating and accomplishing, 'Doing nothing is something.' That was a powerful phrase to let myself let go of the past and my business."

When I look back on leaving Plum, I am certain that it was the right decision. I think about everything I got to do and experience afterward that I wouldn't have had the opportunity for had I still worked there. I wouldn't have gotten to work with Palo and the rest of the REBBL team, including an incredibly supportive board of directors, or to be a part of helping our growers thrive. I wouldn't have been able to say I've fallen passionately in love again with my work. I wouldn't have had the opportunity to serve on other boards, where I've

gotten to know some exceptional people and helped entrepreneurs build great brands. I wouldn't have had the honor
of working at Stanford and teaching at Sonoma State, nurturing future entrepreneurial leaders who will soon be creating great companies that will change the world. I wouldn't
have gotten the chance to kiss my kids after school every day
and hug the bunnies together. I probably wouldn't have had
the opportunity to write this book to support entrepreneurs
and to hopefully start shifting the cultural norms of entrepreneurship. I wish I'd been able to tell all this to the version of
myself who sat in that restaurant with my family feeling so
despondent. My rough transition has made me empathetic,
and my experiences since have made me wise. Leaving isn't
easy, but it's necessary, and the opportunities for growth, for
finding new vessels for your passion, are there for the taking.

When I left Plum to work at Stanford, Patrick and I talked about what else the future might hold for me. It was hard for me to imagine what I would want to do beyond teaching. "Why don't you serve on boards of new companies?" Patrick suggested. "You'd love that."

"Ugh, no way," I told him. "I don't want to have anything to do with business. I'm done."

Everything I've been through since, from trying my hand at stay-at-home mom life, to taking Patrick's advice and serving on boards, to taking the big step of becoming a full-time CEO again, has shown me how much I misunderstood that day when I swore off business. I was tired and I was in fact quite sick. I didn't know that business wasn't to blame.

Recently my fifteen-year-old, Connor, was working on an economics project for school in which he had to improve the financial health of a country—in his case, Peru—and figure out how to make it better. Whereas before he wouldn't have wanted to touch anything business-related with a ten-foot pole, either, he was captivated by this project.

"Mom," he said to me over breakfast. "You're a business-woman. What do you think about developing premium products for other countries?" We talked about what worked for other countries and what didn't. We discussed the exploitation that's happened in Peru due to bad business deals and a corrupt government. Connor was riveted. He had that spark in his eye that I'd seen in my students at Stanford who were so excited to take an idea from their head and make it real. As I explained business principles to Connor, I thought to myself how cool it is to be an entrepreneur. It's intellectual, it's creative, it's collaborative, it's unbelievably satisfying. Successful company or no, those traits are still true of it—if you approach it in the right way, if you don't let your business become intertwined with your sense of self-worth.

Of the many subjects I've covered in this book, self-worth leaves the most lasting footprint. This is the quality that must be the strongest and most fight-ready before you start a company. No matter what's reported during fundraising, quarterly reports, or company valuations, *you* are not a number, *you* are not someone else's scorecard. A number is momentary; a "failure" is momentary. What must endure is a deep feeling that you are living in line with your values, that you are fundamentally grounded. You have to have resilience, and you have to know that you can fall down, get back up, and wipe yourself off, aware that deep down you are okay. Without this strong sense of self-worth, no matter how supportive your partner or your kids or your friends, no matter how bold or humble you are, *you* are at risk, even if your company isn't.

Quite obviously, and as you know from reading this book, I struggled mightily to maintain my self-worth through the ups and downs of business. Though I wouldn't wish an illness like anorexia on anyone, it brought me to face myself in ways I hadn't before. It—and all the experiences that came prior to it—brought me to a place where I had to work on things that I hadn't really examined about the role of entrepreneurship in my life. It brought me to a place where I'm able to treasure the entrepreneurial ride without getting tossed around.

REBBL has given me the opportunity to take all those lessons I learned the hard way and put them to the test. If Plum and Blue Sky were testing grounds where I learned how to fight, REBBL is the proof that those lessons worked, and that it's all been worth it. Although we will do everything in our power to build REBBL into a scalable, enduring company, it may not last forever, and my role at REBBL certainly won't last forever. But that's just the point: it's okay. I have energy, I'm connected to my family and friends, and I love being an entrepreneur.

Oh, and have I mentioned that I'm having the time of my life?

To my collaborator, Jenna Land Free, you killed it. Thank you for brilliantly helping me to find my voice. I feel so lucky to have you as such an unbelievably talented collaborative partner and friend. I couldn't have done this without you. I have so much gratitude for Genoveva Llosa for introducing us and for her input that sparked the shape of this book.

To Stephanie Hitchcock, my editor at HarperCollins, I am beyond grateful to you for believing the vision of this book and then making it sing in a way I never thought possible. Your patient, wise, and thoughtful counsel was always so grounding to me.

To my publisher, Hollis Heimbouch at HarperCollins, and the entire Harper team, including Brian Perrin, Penny Makras, Kathy Schneider, Jonathan Burnham, Tina Andreadis, and Nate Knaebel. You are a killer team and your talent and excitement for this book created magic.

To Margret McBride and Faye Atchison, my agents, thank you for your endless guidance, patience, and tenacity, and for helping this book come to life. Thank you also to Gail Ross for your wise counsel and support.

To Denise Brousseau, who helped the idea for this book

come to the light of day: without your counsel, I wouldn't have even started down this path. And to Michael Dowling, who helped us polish the original proposal that led me to Margret and Faye.

To all the contributors to this book, who were so generous with their time and added critical insights, with a special callout to Steve Blank who has inspired my philosophy on starting companies and teaching. Also, a big thank-you to Dr. Michael Freeman and his groundbreaking study that will help entrepreneurs everywhere.

To the REBBLs, Palo Hawken, Dani Dhanoa, Rachel Hauser, Mike Steele, Jim Arsenault, Matt Briggs, Morgan Geiger, Mike Penta, Greg Fleishman, Kisitina Venegas, Carrie Kosick, Dre Birskovich, Leslie Krasny, Matt Tom, Kris Crown, Brayden Beverage, and the rest of the BVAccel team; the Christie Communications team; Mark Rampolla, Duane Primozich, Kim Perdikou, Dave Batstone, Kuldeep Mulkani, Arif Fazal, Ryan Caldbeck, and the rest of the Circle Up team; Hugh Marquis and all our investors. Every day you inspire me with your passion, creativity, and true grit. You are beautiful people. Thank you for creating and growing and supporting this extremely special company and giving me the honor of being a part of the tribe.

To my Plum cofounder, Neil Grimmer, thank you for being my coparent in the creation of our Nest/Plum baby. Words can't describe my gratitude and awe. Thank you, my friend.

To the rest of the Nest/Plum family, including Bentley Hall, Gigi Chang, Molly Michet, Rachel Skelly, Sangita Forth, Kory Johnston, Sina Caroll, Scott Taylor, Todd Tolboe, Mark Osbourne, Kristal Cerna, Jed Smith, Mike Meyers, Ilya Nykin, Matthew Cowan, Tory Patterson, Jon Owsley, Erika Thorton, Marc-David Bismuth, James Joaquin, Marty Fogelman, Steve

Simon, Todd Steele, Kristin Richmond, Kirsten Tobey, Bill Shen, and so many others along the way, thank you for believing in Nest and growing Plum into a world-class brand. It took your creativity, tenacity, and brilliance in business building to make it possible. I am amazed by each and every one of you.

To the Clif and Company owners, Gary Erickson and Kit Crawford: Your bold vision for what makes a great company and brand changed my life in every way. Thank you for your incredible mentorship and guidance along the journey. To the rest of the Clif tribe, including Kevin Cleary, Michelle and Ewan Ferguson, Bobby Faye, Michelle Steele, Leslie (the Rev) Anderson, Chris Tomsha, Jeff Johnson, Jason Bliss, Rich Boragno, David Jericoff, Tom Richardson, Rosanna Neagle, Sarah Wallace, Jen Freitas, Randy Erickson, Chris Leon, Ron Bryant, Doug Gilmour, Eric and Rochelle Russell, Yana Kushner, Chris Weil, Elizabeth Lombardi, Dean Mayer, Tracy Kelly, Kate Torgersen, Rick Collins, Deven Clemens, Bruce Lymburn, Elysa Hammond, Steve Grossman, Paul McKenzie, Stephen Houghton, Stephanie Wu, Trisha Hutchinson and so many more—your continued commitment and drive to build a five-bottom-line company with mojo is world-changing. I feel so lucky to have been a part of it.

To the visionaries who have inspired me with their dream of a more sustainable future, including Paul Hawken and Hunter Lovins.

To Chuck Holloway and Irv Grousbeck at the Stanford GSB, thank you for your mentorship and for challenging me to think boldly. To my Stanford sister and friend, Bethany Coates, thank you for your friendship, your kindness, and your beautiful smile—you are an uplifting person to be around and so talented. You are going to kill it as an entrepreneur. And thank you to the rest of the GSBers whose insights helped me to understand what drives the most brilliant entrepreneurs: Whitney Flynn, Sharon Hoffman, Maria Jensen, Sara Rosenthal, Arar Hahn, Austin Keissig, Dianna Ziehm, Justin Randolph, William Norvell, Kriss Deiglmeier, Blair Shane, Aileen Sweeney, Suzanne Richards, Courtney Payne, Gina Jordash, Leah Edwards, Nancy Gross, Lisa Sweeney, professors Jennifer Aaker, Maggie Neale, Deb Gruenfeld, JD Schramm, Baba Shiv, Charles O'Reilly, Steve Blank, Steve Ciesinski, Andy Rachleff, Robert Siegal, JD Schramm, Stefanos Zenios, George Foster, Peter DeMarzo, Yossi Feinberg, Jim Ellis, Dean Garth Saloner, the amazing students and alumni, and many more who inspired me along the way.

To the Gardein, thinkThin, Zuke's, Rip van Wafels, Sugar Bowl Bakery, Back to the Roots, the Sustainable Business Council teams, and OSC2, including cofounders Lara Dickinson and Ahmed Rahim, working with you all has been deeply inspiring. It's an honor to have had the opportunity to support your efforts to build beautiful brands and contribute to a more sustainable future.

To the Quaker Oats and General Foods alumni, including Chris Weede, Peter Riccio, Jeff Jacobs, Jeff Lichtman, Jeff Marsh, Sue Wellington, Rachel Orland, Phil Marineau, Cindy Alston, Jeff Shifrin, Ed Several, Jeff Lime, Bob Gamgort, Andy Whitman, Steve Mintz, Irene Rosenfeld, Sue Wellington, Rachel Orland, Phil Marineau, Joel Henry, Maureen Treankler, Matt Bostwick, Shannon McChesney, Lisa Mann, Barbara Eden, Bob Gamgort, and so many others, thank you for teaching me how the best corporations build great brands, manage efficient P&Ls, and lead with integrity,

To my friends at Sonoma State and the Food Business School, including deans Bill Silver and Will Rosenzweig and professors Armand Gilinsky and Kirsten Ely, as well as the wonderful students and alumni, thank you for giving me the opportunity to support aspiring entrepreneurs. At the end of every class I taught, my heart would sing. Your programs are changing the lives of so many people.

To Brandi Hutchings, thank you for helping me organize my life and taking such good care of our family.

To Marissa Harrison and Allison Justice, my fellow bagels, thank you for seeing me when I couldn't see myself and being relentless in grounding me again. Your friendship means the world to me.

To Bev Kingston, Kim Yellen, and Michelle Gottenberg, I have thousands of memories of our times together so long ago. I love that when we talk, time seems to melt away.

To Danae Brooker, my soul sister, I find it impossible to put into words how much your friendship means to me. I can't believe how lucky I am to have a friend as caring and compassionate as you. Thank you for always being there for me. And to the rest of my besties, Andrea Collins, Andrea Compton, and Terri Spath, I'm deeply grateful for your friendship for so many years. Thank you for inspiring me to do this book and for your love and support in helping me come back from the bottom.

Thank you to my cherished friends and extended family members who remind me what's important in life: Chris DeAcutis and Carla Lejeune, Karen Howard and Dave Arute, Jeanne and Ethan Hollander, Susan and Chris Shields, Craig Collins, Brian Justice, George Brooker, Paul Compton, Craig Collins, Jen and Brad Dahme, Christine Carter, Robyn Rutledge, Evelyn Dilsaver, Deb Reisenthal, Colleen Edwards, Mary Huss, John Hahn, Charlie Marinelli, Ben Harrison, Marie and Scott Cross, Susie Chastain, Jean and Dave Thompson, Alice and Ron Lando, Peddie and Leif Arneson, Stacey and Dave Fleece, Evelyn Armstrong Marks and Will Marks, and Yianna and Michael Xenakis; my business school BFFs,

Donna Balinkie, Cynthia Gavenda, Suzanne Aiger, Elaine Clancy, and the rest of the four quarters at Kellogg who are killing it all over the world; the Can Do women; Tone co-owners Monica Anderson and Alyson Dobbert; my trainer, Jenn Haugen, and the rest of the kindhearted community at Tone, including my workout and wine buds, Terri Crawford and Deana Hopper; Elyse, Ken, Marcia, Ed, Marcy, Scott, Erica, Kevin, Jamie, Lindsay, Robyn, John, Bradley, Austin, Rayna, Victor Dann and Jill and Gabreille, as well as Susie and Arthur Geffen, the rest of the Dann and Rosenthal clans, Scott Woodard, the Sheehans, the Zeldeses, the Alumits, and the other wonderful people in my life. I wish I could list you all.

To my parents, Marty and Beverly Zeldes and Stephen and Noleen O'Loughlin: thank you for your loving support and for being role models for a great marriage.

Thank you to my siblings, Steve and Geri Zeldes, Lisa Zeldes, Jan and Peggy Hoeskstra, Pete and Maureen McGee, Steve and Terri O'Loughlin, and Liz O'Loughlin. So many of my greatest memories are of our times together. I love you all.

To my sons, Connor and Gavin O'Loughlin: I am so proud to be your mommy. I am astounded by you and how you are growing up as people with opinions, philosophies, and values. You have taught me how to be a better person. "I love you for always."

And to my husband, Patrick O'Loughlin. I am so deeply in love with you. You are my best friend and my soul mate. Thank you for holding my feet to the ground and reminding me how to find pure joy in just being.

I want to be able to thank everyone who has touched my life and inspired this book. I'm so very sorry if I left anyone out inadvertently.

INDEX

ABOUT THE AUTHOR

SHERYL O'LOUGHLIN earned her MBA from the Kellogg School of Management at Northwestern University. She is the CEO of REBBL super-herb beverages, and she previously served as the CEO of Clif Bar, where she led the concept development and introduction of Luna Bars, and was the cofounder and CEO of Plum Organics. She is the former executive director of the Center for Entrepreneurial Studies at the Stanford Graduate School of Business. She lives in Santa Rosa, California, with her husband, Patrick, and her two sons.